Trouble in the Land of Giving
Australian Charities, Fraud, and the State

—

William De Maria

This work was inspired by and is dedicated to my courageous son Adrian. In valiantly exposing a high order corruption conspiracy in a Brisbane charity, Adrian put himself on the line. In letting his ethics speak he took the gale force of vilification, abuse, lies and threats. The charity has now been cleared out of the fraudsters, one faced court, and Adrian stands tall.

William De Maria

Trouble in the Land of Giving

Australian Charities, Fraud, and the State

PALAVER 2020

Author's note

After 20 rejections of my manuscript by book publishers, it is fair to say I was deep into my J.K. Rowling moment. The sky turned blue again when two days after submission, I received a very positive response from Paul Komesaroff, the director of Palaver. Unlike other publishers who opened my manuscript as if it was a box of brown snakes, Professor Komesaroff, and fellow editor, Dr. Sally Gardner, did not see danger, but opportunity.

Palaver is a brand-new imprint, and an exciting new entry into Australian publishing. They are here because, in their own words; "Our organization has come into existence in response to a widely perceived sense that academic publishing today has been compromised by the development of global monopolies and the penetration of corporatist and managerialist values into both universities and the industry itself. These tendencies have eroded the independence of much academic publishing and have shifted the focus of editorial decision-making to commercial objectives".

I thank Paul and Sally for allowing me to be part of this brave new venture into ethical publishing.

William De Maria

TROUBLE IN THE LAND OF GIVING
Australian Charities, Fraud, and the State
A Palaver Book

ISBN-13: 978-0-9752352-5-6

For additional information, bulk or educational purchases, and other resources, please contact Ethica Projects, Pty. Ltd
c/o Paul Komesaroff: paul.komesaroff@monash.edu
First Palaver Edition published January 2020
Graphic design and typesetting: Ian Robertson
Typeface: Tiempos — Kris Sowersby / Klim Type Foundry

www.palaver.com
Palaver is an imprint of Ethica Projects, Pty Ltd.
10 Barnato Grove Armadale Victoria 3143 Australia

Contents

Foreword

I've known Bill De Maria since the 1990s. He did pioneering research on whistleblowing, from the point of view of whistleblowers. I was involved in Whistleblowers Australia, including as president 1996–1999, and Bill's work loomed large. Back then, Bill and I had many exchanges about whistleblowing. I've often cited his important book *Deadly Disclosures* (Wakefield 1999). He was passionate about injustice and about the failure of institutions to address it. He still is.

Trouble in the Land of Giving makes a valuable contribution to Australian debates and policy from two particular angles. The historical treatment of government welfare provision, especially its neoliberal retreat, offers insights not available by simply looking at contemporary charity and need. The second angle is fraud, both the illegal sort of direct stealing and the legal sort (not officially called fraud) of tax and other rules allowing the rich to benefit from charitable giving. Insights from Bill's case studies, such as the Shane Warne Foundation and the epic saga of Eman Sharobeem, are especially disturbing because so many people make donations in good faith, yet too much of the money fails to get to those who need it most.

Bill's work is rigorous in its scholarship, as shown in his detailed accounts of the cases he studies. Unlike most academic writing, though, Bill has a style that is engaging through a combination of hard-hitting analysis and vivid language, and the result is prose that is unusually accessible outside the academy.

Bill is an iconoclast. I say this in admiration. His career has not been easy because of his outspoken views. His capabilities as a scholar combined with his willingness to criticise both governments and business make his contributions especially valuable. *Trouble in the Land of Giving* is an initial expedition into uncharted waters. There is so much secrecy that only a great deal more work of this kind will reveal the full extent of the problems. Some of the cases Bill describes are ongoing. However, it would be a mistake to wait for the outcomes, because they are likely to be many years away.

Bill has shown the way. Others need to follow.

Brian Martin
Emeritus Professor of Social Sciences
University of Wollongong NSW 2522
bmartin@uow.edu.au, http://www.bmartin.cc/

Everybody knows that the dice are loaded
Everybody rolls with their fingers crossed
Everybody knows that the war is over
Everybody knows the good guys lost
Everybody knows the fight was fixed
The poor stay poor, the rich get rich
That's how it goes
Everybody knows

Everybody knows that the boat is leaking
Everybody knows that the captain lied
Everybody got this broken feeling
Like their father or their dog just died

...

Leonard Cohen "Everybody knows"

Abbreviations

ABC Australian Broadcasting Corporation
ACCC Australian Competition and Consumer Commission
ACL Australian Christian Lobby
ACNC Australian Charities and Not-for-profits Commission
ADB Australian Dictionary of Biography
ASIC Australian Securities and Investments Corporation
ATO Australian Taxation Office
CAV Community Affairs Victoria
CFO Chief Financial Officer
CPPC Catholic Psychiatry Pastoral Care
CRC Community Relations Commission
DPP Director of Public Prosecutions
FACS Family and Community Services
FTSE Financial Times Stock Exchange
ICAC Independent Commission Against Corruption
IPA Institute of Public Affairs
ISO International Standards for Organisation
IWHS Immigrant Women's Health Service
KMF KordaMentha Forensic
NAB National Australia Bank
NESH Non-English Speaking Housing Women's Scheme
NFP Not-for-profit (organisation)
NGO Non-government Organisation
PAF Private Ancilliary Fund
PAYG Pay As You Go taxation
PFRA Public Fundraising Regulatory Association
QSL Queensland Sugar Limited
RCACQS Royal Commission into Aged Care Quality and Safety
RSL Returned Services League
SBS Special Broadcasting Service
SES Smart Employment Solutions
SWSLHD South Western Sydney Local Health District

Introduction

Australians are a big-hearted people. Currently eleven charities are registered every business day in Australia.[1] There are more charities in Australia now than at any time in its white history. Is this just a function of increased population? Perhaps. It may also be a bugle call on our troubled times.

If Rip Van Winkle went to sleep in Australia in 1943 (note the date) and woke now, his first comment may be, "Where has the bloody welfare state gone"? Mr. Winkle took his slumber just as the Commonwealth Government was designing a post-war grand scale welfare state, as I explain in Chapter One. On waking he is aghast to see so many businesses running user-pay and tax-paid welfare services. It's business, business, business now. He cannot believe the size of the big charities. He sees queues for government services everywhere. He sees poverty on a scale he never experienced. Someone had to explain to him why so many people are sleeping rough. He had a lot of questions about a phrase he was hearing everywhere: "mental health". When told, he was astounded at the high suicide rates among young people and he could not see where the services were for them. He remembers the soup kitchens from his younger days in the Great Depression. But now, when he looks out on the street, people are lining up for second-hand food, second-hand toys and second-hand clothing. Charities are everywhere! A sadness comes over him. He wants to go back to sleep.

What Mr Winkle does not get (he's been asleep after all) is that this intense charitable activity is a grave populist response to the dramatic explosion in unmet social need. What Toynbee calls the "scars of austerity".[2] We should also talk about the scars of inequality. The great myth we just cannot seem to give up on is that Australia is a world model of egalitarianism. I won't burden this point with loads of confirming research. Rather, I will share two images with you. In the first, Alan Joyce, the *wunderkind* Qantas CEO, is sitting (first class?) in one of his planes. He looks happy, vital, ready to go. Why shouldn't he? Joyce has just topped the list of Australia's highest paid CEOs in 2018, taking home $23.9 million, 275 times the average worker's salary.[3] That's one image. Then there is Lisa Carberry, 48. Her weekly income is $343. The current relative poverty line for a single person is $430 pw.[4] Lisa is living $100 under the poverty line. Her income is made up of: Newstart, $277.85 a week, her energy supplement: $4.40 a week, her rent assistance is $65.85 a week and her pharmaceutical allowance is $6.20 a week. She has regular expenses of $304.20. Her rent is $149 a week, her car repayments are $136.15 a week (paid monthly), her phone is $11.55 a week (paid monthly) and her Robodebt is $7.50 a week. This leaves Lisa a sum of $5.60 a day to live on after she has paid for food and utilities.[5]

Two people, smiling Alan and gloomy Lisa, looking at you, both in their own ways, daring you to call Australia egalitarian. The unforgivable disparities of wealth are matched with the disparities in government treatment. Evidence will come forward in the pages ahead to say that governments care for and look after the Joyces of this world far more than they do the Carberrys.

The tsunami of want has produced what I call, somewhat tongue in cheek, the golden age of charity. Charities are flourishing, if not in performance, certainly in activity, doing the heavy lifting for governments who drift along in egregious indifference to this social need.

One thing for sure is that the period we are in now in Australia is a charity version of rush hour. It really looks like chaos. There are no centralising themes, no sense of charities working together, and certainly no sense that this massive charitable output is making a difference. It's more of a feeling of just holding the line against a tsunamic surge in want and despair.

Take homelessness. As the number of people without permanent shelter rises to crueller heights so does the number of charities working in that area. Shouldn't this relationship be an inverse one? The most recent reliable figures on homelessness in Australia show it increasing by 14% between the 2011 and the 2016 censuses.[6] For every 10,000 people, 50 are homeless and more than 43,500 people homeless are under twenty five years of age.[7] Yet, and remarkably so, 46,716 registered charities claim that combatting homelessness is one of their core missions.[8] In other words, 81% of all charities registered with the national regulator in mid-2019 *say* they are working in the homeless area. Incredible! There is something very wrong here and it would take a massive research project to get to the bottom of it. Charity fraud, fallacious reporting and non-performance by charities, along with the charity regulator's reliance on self-reporting from charities as to what they do (to secure luscious tax advantages) should be targets of a lot more research and political action.

Charities, on these figures, are obviously performing abysmally in the homeless area. One area however where there is a lot of performance is in the intense, and at times bullying competition for the unpredictable donor dollar. Butcher recently called this competition the new "welfare arms race".[9] The current charity donor scene is either a glitzy cabaret of big charities filling skip bins of money through slick pantomime tricks such as CEO sleepouts or an abundance of earnest small charities scratching out an existence like modern day sack-clothed mendicants.[10] It's the mega charities and the lemonade stands on the same patch.

Charities: the New Welfare State?

One of the intentions of this book is to show that this hotbed of charitable action *and inaction* is a direct result of governments having abandoned their traditional welfare obligations to their citizens. This proposition is naturally going to require some defence, particularly in light of the fact that Commonwealth social security and welfare services at the time of writing account for 35% of Australian Government expenses, with the forward estimate predicting that will mean $191.8 billion in 2019–20.[11] On the face of it, this spending does not look like the government has walked away from its welfare mandate.

There are several elements to the back story that give quite a different perspective on these so-called massive state welfare expenditures.[12]

First, the latest government figures, detailed in the chart opposite, show that the key drivers of this growth will come from only two programs: the National Disability Insurance Scheme and provision for the aged. Commentary on welfare expenditure usually sidelines this point in favour of a misrepresented view that such expenditure is about various income supports for working-age people generally.

Secondly, it must also be recognised that government welfare budgets are always vulnerable to expansions and retractions. But these changes are never across the board. When welfare spending increases it is usually in areas tracking major demographic changes (e.g. our aging population) or where a social policy enjoys bipartisan support (e.g. the National Disability Insurance Scheme).

Thirdly, the size of government welfare budgets always makes them targets for savings measures, particularly in times of budget deficits.[13] That's the unpredictable thing about these big welfare budgets. There are always winners and losers. Thus, a homeless service running on government payments has its funding suddenly cut and must hastily re-jig its operations to become dependent on goodwill donations from the public or cease operating. The only constant here is that the homeless stay homeless.

Finally, the so-called big welfare budgets hide a gross inequity in social provision. I speak of tectonic plate changes to the public-private mix in the provision of services. Cruel spikes in youth suicides and flood proportion statistics on rising rates of depression and anxiety (to name two) are overwhelming charities who not only find themselves filling old service voids but colonising emerging need because governments simply refuse to respond with adequate public resources. In all but the demographically driven responses and those few initiatives attracting bipartisan support (mentioned above) government social intervention is now well into stagnation or significant retraction. Where once charities entered the field because it was the right thing to do, charities now enter the field because it's the only thing to do.

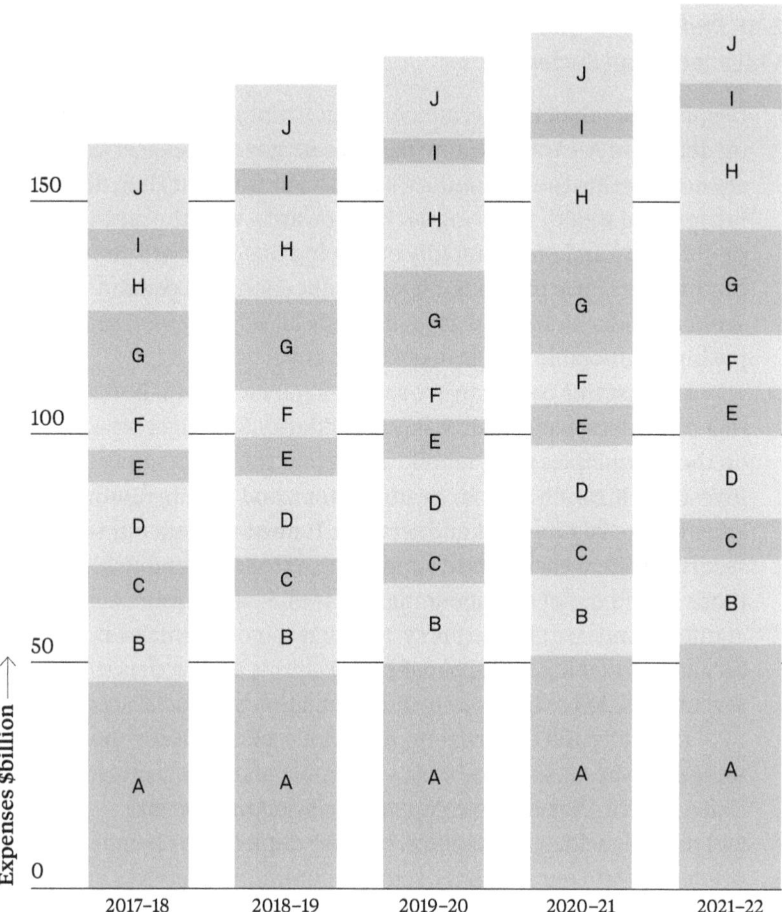

A — Age Pension and income support for seniors
B — Disability Support Pension
C — Carer payments
D — Family tax benefit
E — Child-care fee assistance
F — Job-seeker income support
G — Aged Care and other assistance for the aged
H — NDIS and other disability services or programs
I — Assistance to veterans and dependants
J — Other welfare programs and administration

Figure 1. Estimated Australian Government expenses on social security and welfare, $b. Source: Australian Government, *Budget strategy and outlook: budget paper no. 1: 2018–19*, pp. 6–23, 6–27.

The day-in, day-out grind by charities filling old service voids and working in new areas of emerging need is well voiced in the 2018 *Budget Priorities Statement* from the National Office of the St. Vincent de Paul Society:

> Despite more than two decades of uninterrupted economic growth, inequality in Australia is growing and core government services are not meeting the community's needs. Far from trickling down, income and wealth are being sucked upwards, with the growth in productivity and profits rapidly outpacing wages growth. Sustained funding cuts have placed our health, education, and community services under strain, and gaps in our social security system are pushing vulnerable people deeper into poverty ...
>
> Against this backdrop, we are calling for a Federal Budget that prioritises justice, fairness and solidarity. A Budget based on these principles must rebuild and repair the social safety net, invest in education and our health system, and restore funding to essential social programs and services. It must reorient our social security system back toward supporting, rather than punishing, those locked out of the labour market. It must also ensure a more equitable and sustainable tax system that removes unfair tax breaks and loopholes that benefit the wealthy, and secures the revenue needed to fund our health, education and social services.
>
> Critically, the Government must not seek to balance the Budget on the backs of the most vulnerable and disadvantaged. Delivering further cuts to company taxes and income tax will not only widen inequalities, but also deplete the revenue needed to fund our hospitals, schools, community services and public infrastructure.
>
> Tax cuts will inevitably lead to more cuts to essential service and supports. And if those spending cuts are directed to public services, shrinking the social safety net, and shifting to 'user-pays' systems in essential services such as healthcare and education, it is inevitable that the wealth gap in Australia will increase and become further entrenched.[14]

Governments for the Rich, Charities for the Poor?

Let me take this point about tax cuts a little further. New modelling from the Australia Institute shows that the recently re-elected Morrison Government will spend more on tax cuts for high income earners than on the Pharmaceutical Benefits Scheme.[15] The cuts, outlined in the 2019 Budget mean that a person earning $50,000 will receive a tax cut of $1205 and a person earning $200,000 or more will get a tax cut of $11,640. Under this, at the time of writing, unlegislated arrangement low income earners will pay 1.7% more tax and high-income earners will be paying 4% less tax. That's $77 billion in tax cuts to the rich over the next 10 years.[16] Keep walking. Nothing new to see here. Just a wealth-centred government doing what wealth-centred governments do.[17]

The argument so far has sought to expose significant weaknesses in the official proposition that the government's 35% of budget commitment to social security and welfare is proof it is meeting its social obligations. Worse, the social security system is morphing into an American-type user pay social insurance scheme where the low to middle level earners pay for their own welfare and the welfare of the rich.[18] So what are the rich up to when it comes to charity?

"Stop talking about philanthropy and start talking about taxes". With this statement Dutch academic, Rutger Bregman, blew the lid off the 2019 World Economic Forum in Davos, Switzerland. It did not take Bregman long to be the most reviled person in the room. In front of an audience of wealthy and powerful business chiefs, Bregman took aim at billionaires for pushing "stupid philanthropy schemes":

> This is my first time at Davos, and I've found it quite a bewildering experience to be honest. I mean, 1,500 private jets were flown in here to hear Sir David Attenborough speak about how we're wrecking the planet. Almost no one raises the real issue of tax avoidance, and of the rich just not paying their fair share. I mean, it feels like I'm at a firefighter's conference and no one is allowed to speak about water. We can talk for a very long time about all these stupid philanthropy schemes, we can invite Bono once more, but come on, we've got to be talking about taxes. That's it, taxes, taxes, taxes. All the rest is bullshit.[19]

Bregman's diatribe was targeted at the non-tax paying rich who use philanthropy for tax avoidance and reputational enhancement. According to Harvard University's 2018 *Global Philanthropy Report*, 1 per cent of the world's population now own half of the world's wealth — a significant leap from 43% of the world's wealth in 2008 — while 10% of the global population still lives on less than $2.80 a day.[20] In research details to follow it will be revealed that the rich in Australia (as elsewhere in the world) are not just quarantining their wealth in offshore tax shelters, they are now starting to hoard it in philanthropic trusts cleverly set up by their all too smart tax lawyers. The rich are structuring their philanthropic trusts as profit-making enterprises by taking full advantage of every tax break available to them.

So not only is the frenetic charity landscape that I have sketched (with more detail to follow) a structural response to the harsh paradox of rising need and retracting government, it also appears that we are entering an age of philanthropy where increasing numbers of wealthy individuals, families and corporations set up foundations "with unintended consequences, like sidelining the responsibilities of governments".[21]

We have already briefly approached the issue of the tax benefits to people who give to charities and the tax benefits of charities who are registered with the regulator. These tax-incentives reduce the revenue that would otherwise be available for government welfare projects. Tax concessions to charities and tax concessions to donors amount to over $1.3 billion per year.[22] That's a lot of money diverted

Paul Ramsey Foundation	$83.1 million
Ian Potter Foundation	$35.4 million
Graham and Louise Tuckwell Foundation	$30 million
Minderoo Foundation	$18.7 million
Lowy Foundation	$18 million
Kinghorn Foundation	$15 million
Susan and Isaac Wakil Foundation	$14.7 million
Myer Foundation and Sidney Myer Foundation	$13.3 million
Packer Family Foundation	$10.3 million
Clive Berghofer Foundation	$10 million

Figure 2. Top Ten Australian Philanthropic Foundations
Source: *Australian Financial Review,* 25 April 2018. https://www.afr.com/afr-magazine/philanthropy-50-australias-top-private-givers-20180313-h0xemk

from use by governments. I propose certain reforms in the last chapter that deal with this sequestered public wealth.

Although we may laud wealthy individuals who give away their money for the benefit of society (see Figure 2), Reich says:

> ... such generosity not only isn't the unassailable good we think it to be but might also undermine democratic values and set back aspirations of justice. Big philanthropy is often an exercise of power, the conversion of private assets into public influence. And it is a form of power that is largely unaccountable, often perpetual, and lavishly tax advantaged. The affluent—and their foundations—reap vast benefits even as they influence policy without accountability. And small philanthropy, or ordinary charitable giving, can be problematic as well. Charity, it turns out, does surprisingly little to provide for those in need and sometimes worsens inequality.[23]

This chart of the top ten philanthropic organisations (Private Ancillary Funds [PAFs]) in Australia needs to be read against the brutal statistic that about 40% of Australia's wealthiest give little or nothing to charity.[24] As I said, those who do, usually structure their giving in tax- smart ways to squeeze the greatest financial benefits for themselves from their philanthropic efforts.[25]

The Australian Taxation Office refuses to reveal the number of philanthropic organisations in Australia that are structured for tax purposes.[26] However we do know from Treasury figures that foundations receive generous subsidies in the form of tax benefits of at least 45 cents in every philanthropic dollar![27] The tax benefits PAFs received between 2001 and 2009 totalled $935.468 million. This is *more than double* the $461.77 million amount PAFs returned to the community in grants.[28] These astounding figures suggest philanthropic organisations are making a profit from their giving! These trusts, in other words, can be nothing but extensions of profiteering corporate power.

Because we don't have the "glass pockets" transparency regime that American philanthropic trusts must adhere to, we know very little about the operations of Australian philanthropic trusts, notwithstanding they draw in loads of public finance. Try searching for public documents of the Packer Family Foundation and you will see what I mean.

Charitable organisations and philanthropic trusts separately embody the rapidly emerging privatisation of government responsibility. This is not a simple point about outsourcing. Governments are not just turning over their welfare responsibilities to business-modelled charities, they are *abdicating* these responsibilities. This relinquishment is probably not reversible and may well be unconstitutional.[29]

Changing the Private–Public Mix Forever?

So, while charity is a significant outcome of the rolled-back state, it also carries a troubling DNA. In structural terms, charity has been caught up in a subtle insurrection against the notion of *égalité*. Crazily, it's an insurrection from above. There has never been an instance in the last fifty years when people have massed on the streets and called out: "What do we want?" "Privatisation"! "When do we want it?" "Now!" The retraction in the Australian service state in favour of pro-business models of service delivery was engineered by successive governments who stopped listening to the people and cravenly took instructions from big business.[30]

Enter the new army of good people running all manner of charities filling the moral and service voids left by governments. Silently, and without much debate, charitable action is, by responding to this shameful government inertia, unintentionally changing the private-public mix forever.[31] Egalitarianism, born behind the barricades of the French Revolution, is the great *sine qua non* of democratic societies and is supposed to flow on into social policy. It is behind all forms of governance that strive for equal rights, one person-one vote and equality before the law.[32]

Charity, it may be a surprise to hear, is unsympathetic to this project. Charity is not egalitarian. Charity provides partial, unstable and highly discriminatory responses when universal action (the "public" in the public-private mix) is called for. Charities bring food to the poor without necessarily addressing poverty. If, in the rare event they do speak out, they find themselves in trouble with governments, as I show in Chapter Two. Charities give shelter without necessarily tackling homelessness and the inequities in the housing market. Charities, in other words, fill gaps when deep transformative change is required.[33]

I make this point carefully and with great sympathy for charities because raw need on the streets cannot wait for the "transformation". Something must be done now, and charities are stepping into the moral vacuum and doing exactly that. My point is a structural one. The more widespread and potent the gap-filling charity model becomes the less demand there is for governments to return to their primary obligations.[34] A recent *New Statesman* article, tellingly titled "Mind the Gap. How Charities are Mopping Up after the Government's Failure to Care", concentrated on the explosion of small local charities in the UK helping people just get the basics in a society where the poor continue to be bashed by the welfare cuts under Conservative rule. Dawn Wilson, the founder of the Durham Food Bank, was interviewed for the *New Statesman* article. Wilson got the idea for the Food Bank after seeing a woman crying in a local shoe shop. The woman was overheard to say to her young son, "It's your sister's turn. I am sorry son".[35]

Yes, charity is a gap filler. But there is more. Charities depend on donor responses that are spasmodic, erratic and emotional when, at risk of labouring the point, rational long-term social planning and action is needed. Charities also alter the accountability context. Government provision should be openly accountable to the people. Charity provision, on the other hand, is privately and essentially responsive to donors, particularly in circumstances where reputational damage must be avoided. But it is not accountable to donors.[36] The relationship between people who give money particularly to the big charities and the professionals in those charities who allocate this money across programs remains un-researched. There is anecdotal evidence which suggests that this relationship is not all that it seems.

Catholic Psychiatry Pastoral Care (CPPC) was established in Brisbane 35 years ago by a Catholic priest and a Catholic laywoman.[37] Its purpose, which it has achieved brilliantly, is to pastorally minister to the needs of psychiatrically vulnerable people through a huge Catholic volunteer commitment, fundraising and donor support.[38] After the Queensland Government unexpectedly cut off funding CPPC was forced to establish closer links with Centacare, the umbrella organisation for Catholic welfare. Recently a wealthy donor and his wife, grateful for the care their disabled son has been given at CPPC for many years, wanted to fund a new kitchen in the day centre where clients ("members") receive cooked meals. The donor was told that the decision to fund the new kitchen was not his to make. The decision as to how to spend his donation would be made by staff from the Archdiocese of Brisbane Catholic Foundation.[39] So, there can be awkward relationships between donors and charities in the distribution of charity dollars.

The actual harvesting of the donation dollar also needs our attention. This harvesting is all askew because it depends on how effectively charities flirt with the donor market. Slick advertising companies are brought in and social need is packaged and promoted like biscuits. Ads and campaigns pull at our heart strings and force us to choose between the benefaction of a homeless charity or one that rehouses greyhounds. This is a market of vicissitudinous morality. What triggers a downpour of donations one year will be a dry riverbed the next. If it's not the cute images of doe-eyed Labrador puppies, it's the confronting images of the bruised face of a domestic violence victim. It's the millionaire prostate cancer survivor who endows a medical research facility engaged in finding a cure for that cancer. The millionaire has chosen to donate to a cause close to his heart. But this is not necessarily the cancer that is producing the greatest need. Only a government is capable of egalitarian redistribution. There is no moral constancy in the redistribution of wealth for charitable purposes. It is whim governed.[40] How did we get to this? Simple answer: through the privatisation of government social responsibility.

This privatisation started in the 1970s. Back then Australia was a smaller, more benevolent and kinder place.[41] Although on its last legs, a soft socialist approach to government in the 1970s still meant wide social provision funded through general revenue. Fast forward to now. A dystopian place for the homeless, the poor and the mentally ill and a utopian palace for the tax-shielded rich. Mad Max meets St. Vincent de Paul.[42] Successive governments have found new ways and new arguments to justify their retreat from their fundamental obligation to care for and nurture their citizens. The voids left by these retreats have been filled, when it is profitable to do so, by the carpet baggers of business (remember Eddy Groves and ABC Learning Centres?),[43] and when it is unprofitable, by the hard-pressed religious and secular charities.

Governments now are like the rich couple shooing beggars away from their door. Governments now don't really want to be too messed up in the charity business. They are quite happy to encourage other entities to do these jobs. A bit like hiring people to move the beggars on. So dependent have governments become on the private sector that when welfare scandals erupt in this sector, governments, more than not, are slow to respond, even defiantly deaf to the complaints.

The Bupa short case in Chapter Two demonstrates this point. The case is around abuse and neglect in the healthcare group's network of nursing homes. While worrying reports were reaching the government it perversely awarded a major health contract to Bupa. One of the last decisions to be made by Defence Minister, Christopher Pyne, before he retired from parliament, was to announce that Bupa would replace Medibank as the Australian Defence Force's healthcare contractor from 1 July 2019. This example of patronage in the face of scandal prompts us to ask the question: what does errant business have to do to get itself out of favour with a business-loving government?

These are some of the issues. But there are a lot more to consider. The purpose of this book is to set off on a voyage of exploration and visit some of the significant sites in the troubled land of giving. We will start with a history of charity in Australia and end with anecdotally rich cases of charity fraud.

Chapter Sketches

In Chapter One, *Australian Charity: History of a Cold Place,* the historical scene is set. For various reasons explained in the chapter, Australian charities languished from the point of white settlement to the first great depression in the 1890s. The mountain of misery that this depression caused: unemployment, hunger, illness, despair, showed that only through government action would these conditions be challenged and eradicated. The full florescence of the idea came about during World War II, in the remarkable and historically unrepeatable partnership between Prime Minster Curtin and his loyal Treasurer, Ben Chifley. Together they crafted the national welfare scheme and, for this reason and others, charities took a back seat. For a generation after

World War II white citizens felt they were living securely under a Scandinavian type social security umbrella.

Unbeknownst to the government of the time, including the great post-war reconstruction bureaucrat, H.C. Coombs, a virus had entered the body politic.[44] By the 1970s, this virus had spread under deceptive euphemisms such as "economic rationalism", "economic liberalism" and "market economy".[45] These were just Social Darwinian codes for small government, big business, minimally fettered capitalism, consumers not citizens, and the commercialisation of *all* services including welfare, health and education.

The government was going away, out of the lives of the vulnerable. But social need stayed and became more obvious (think homelessness). Something had to be done. Thus, the golden age of charities emerged. In one sense this is a unique social movement. It taps into the natural benevolence of people, not all people, but enough to start building services and catering for the vast spectrum of unmet need. It also taps into a new social assertiveness. People of good will know that waiting for governments to pick up need is often waiting forever. We are hearing less and less the phrase, once common in social discourse, "What is the government going to do about it"? People are getting the message and getting on with it.

In Chapter Two, *Australian Charities: Size, Shape and Controversies,* the current sector, shaped by the historical forces detailed in the previous chapter, is weighed and measured. Some surprises here. The charity sector is much bigger than people might think. In 2015–16 it generated $152.4 billion in income. Not as large as mining ($179.3 billion) but bigger than agriculture ($100.9 billion). We know there are over 600,000 not-for-profit organisations in Australia, of which there are only about 58,000 charities registered with the ACNC. These are the not-for-profits that took the bait marked "tax-free donations".

The disparity in size between the charities is almost unbelievable. The chapter leads evidence that shows that the top ten charities in 2016 had a combined revenue that year of $19 billion. To put that in perspective, in the same year, Australia's largest bank, the ethically challenged Commonwealth Bank, had revenue of $26.2 billion. While these huge sums are generated by big charity, the chapter also reveals that over 10,000 small registered charities in Australia in 2016 earnt no income whatsoever.

The chapter then responds to an emerging issue in the sector at the time of writing to do with advocacy charities. The Morrison Government and the Turnbull Government before that, have a real problem with advocacy charities even though they only constitute .08% of registered charities. This is articulated in the discussion of the registered charity, Catholic Education Melbourne, which has recently been given a show cause why its charitable status should not be cancelled because of the organisation's alleged activities in a recent election.

Finally, in this chapter, attention is drawn to what must be the most significant controversy facing the delivery of charity today in Australia. The controversy sits within the dominant charity-business paradigm which is considered here to be fundamentally flawed. In short, the business mindset has taken over the delivery of charity. We see it in the new language: where once the discourse in charities tinkled with words like "care", "need" and "compassion", the new discourse clangs with words like "markets", "profit", efficiency", "value for money", "eligibility", "fiscal responsibility" and "targets". We don't have to wait on the report from the Royal Commission into Aged Care Quality and Safety to understand that the very reason for the Commission's existence is to respond to a crisis triggered by the flawed charity-business paradigm which refuses to believe that there is something terribly contradictory about making a buck from vulnerability.[46]

In Chapter Three, *Charity Fraud and its Regulation*, the analysis moves on from the metrics of charities to the darker aspect of charity fraud. Charity fraud, as an insidious form of stealing, is examined from several angles, starting with the vulnerabilities of charitable organisations. Statistics from Scamwatch, operated by the Australian Competition and Consumer Commission are used to reveal disturbing levels of charity fraud in Australia. The chapter then analyses the numerous ways charity fraud is carried out.

From there, the chapter considers how the very act of winning the scarce charity dollar can produce fraudulent outcomes. Mention is made of a multi-million-dollar class action filed in 2016 against leading fundraiser, Appco Group Australia, which has raised funds for organisations such as the Starlight Foundation and Surf Life Saving Australia. The company is accused of sham contracting and bullying charity collectors.

Discussion then moves to the new national charity regulator, the Australian Charities and Not-for-profits Commission. While the Commission, established in 2012, is still in its building period the signs are not good. Parliament did not give it ACCC type prosecution initiating powers. The Commission's investigations never see the light of day and it is resourced in a way that gives rise to the response: "You can't be serious". In a decision that is at best quirky and at worse administratively detrimental, the government has allowed the new Chair of the Australian Charities and Not-for-profits Commission, Gary Johns, to remain in a one-person office in his home city of Brisbane while the rest of his 107 staff toil it out in the Commission's Melbourne base.

Finally in this chapter, I offer a unique biography of Gary Johns. I do this because he is a man of his times in the sense that his career is an unusually clear personification of how business got the ascendancy in charitable provision.

The next three chapters get into the hard case material. A new three-part typology of charity failure is offered. Charities are classified as either *celebrity charities, iconic charities* or *key player charities*. Using both government and media sources, the Shane Warne Foundation is studied as an example of how deeply flawed the celebrity charity model is. With access to an important anti-corruption investigation, the New South Wales RSL is case studied as an example of iconic charity fraud. Finally, a key player charity, where a rogue operator created havoc, is studied using police and court documents. At the time of writing, Amanda Kate Smith was still in jail for charity fraud at her previous place of employment, Smart Employment Solutions.

These typologies are not offered as hard and fast categories. There is a lot of porosity between them. The main thing is to try to understand different forms of charity failure. Tolstoy, in his novel *Anna Karenina*, famously said, "All happy families are alike; each unhappy family is unhappy in its own way". This observation underpins the logic behind the typology. Every charity is similar. When they fail, they do so in different ways. Celebrity charity failure comes about because razzamatazz overtakes the charitable objectives. Iconic charity failure comes about because crooks are shielded from scrutiny within a charity that has a long history of community service and is trusted and loved for that. Key player charity failure simply comes down to one central person in the charity who goes rogue, takes advantage of serious audit lapses and plunders the scarce resources of the charity, even to the point of destroying the charity reputationally and financially.

The final chapter has been left for a rare, intensive insight into charity fraud. This is because the matter profiled has been the subject of lengthy judicial proceedings. Eman Sharobeem at the Immigrant Women's Health Service (IWHS) faced a formal investigation by the NSW Independent Commission against Corruption (ICAC).[47] She was found to have engaged in seriously corrupt conduct and is awaiting a decision by the NSW Director of Public Prosecutions as to whether she goes to trial.

With the voyage through the land of giving complete, a retrospect of the travels replaces a traditional conclusion. In *Hindsight* the main themes captured throughout the book are revisited. *Hindsight* tries to offer a tighter coupling of the main features of this troubled land, although readily acknowledging that more research is needed. In this troubled land live the poor, the mentally ill, the homeless, the victims of violence, and many more. Their existence brings us collective dishonour. Surveyed from another angle, we see it is a land of Australians of compassion, working tirelessly in numerous charitable organisations. Then there are the greedy carpetbaggers, businesspeople fully briefed about our tax concession laws, looking to make a buck out of vulnerability (see the Bupa Group vignette). Also staking their claims in this troubled land are the fraudsters, as depicted in the fraud case studies, who, answering the base siren calls of capitalism, steal charitable funds for private lifestyle purchases. The land also hosts very powerful anti-charity enclaves that rant about too many public funds going to the poor and otherwise disadvantaged (think Institute of Public Affairs). Finally, there is the charity regulator, the Australian Charities and Not-for-profits Commission, small, powerless, clueless and confused.

The troubled land of giving is, from a research perspective, an un-reconnoitred land. Charity is yet to become a serious research topic in Australia. *Hindsight* presents a case for greater insights into the triangulation between charities, fraud and the state.

Chapter One
Australian Charity: History of a Cold Place

For charity is cold in the multitude of possessions and the rich are covetous of their crumbs.

Christopher Smart, English poet, 1758.[48]

This chapter offers a time-lapsed context, rather than a conventional historical analysis of Australian charity.[49] It looks at how, over time, private charitable endeavour and government social provision have been *inversely* bound together. When government welfare activity is positive, generous and effective, private charity is patchy, local and poorly endowed. The inverse is also true. When governments cut back on their social obligations or fail to adequately respond to emerging areas of need, charities rush to fill the voids and, in doing so, the charity arms race, as was previously considered, starts in earnest. Therefore, the historical details in this chapter are picked to emphasise that the history of Australian charity has always been a history of the tug-of-war between two propositions: private charity and public welfare.

A recent JB Were study of the number of charities in Australia since 1800 shows low level, almost flatline growth from 1800 to the 1890s when Australia had its first major depression. From then until around the 1970s there is moderate growth in the number of charities in Australia. After that date and until now the growth of charities soars like compound interest.[50] This exponential growth, as I will explain, coincides with the effective neo-conservative attacks on government welfare spending that started in the 1970s, when government social provision reached its zenith under the Labor prime ministership of Gough Whitlam.[51]

Before Federation

The colonial governments in Australia inherited from their British masters the cold charity ideological framework that had existed since the *Poor Relief Act 1601*. Popularly known as the *Elizabethan Poor Law*, the 1601 Act created a new public benevolence system that would last four hundred years, until the beginning of the twentieth century.[52]

By the Elizabethan period the two common sources of charity, the monasteries and the medieval social structure were breaking down. Something was needed to replace these as ways of dealing with mountain size poverty, famines, plagues and other calamities.

The *Elizabethan Poor Law* provided for the impotent poor (people who could not work because they were "lame, impotent, old, blind") to be cared for at parish level alms houses or in poor houses. The able-bodied poor were to be set to work in houses of industry, similar in some ways to the prison industries we have today. The idle poor and vagrants, perceived more as a social threat, were sent to houses of correction, or even prison. Pauper children would become apprentices.

Under these new Elizabethan arrangements, the levels of generosity varied wildly, depending on political and economic realities at the parish level, as each parish under the Act was responsible for its "own poor".[53] The "charity" that was dispensed was cold, punitive, stingy, judgemental and arbitrary. It came in two forms: indoor and outdoor relief. Indoor relief, in the form of food, shelter and some medical attention was offered within the workhouses and alms houses. Outdoor relief was offered outside a workhouse. This could come in the form of money, food or even clothing, in exchange for the poor person's labour. Anyone with a cursory understanding of the Australian social security system would recognise that this outdoor model is still alive and well in current government social policy.

The 1601 *Poor Law* provided for overseers of the poor. These early versions of the modern social worker were authorised to apply intuition, bias and cruelty to distinguish between the "deserving poor" and the "undeserving poor". This debate is as fresh today as it was at the time of its Elizabethan inception. Ask any Centrelink client.

From settlement in 1788 to the middle of the nineteenth century, charitable provision, both governmental and voluntary, was slow to develop. Lawrence speculates that charity in the Australian colonies was weak compared with nineteenth-century Britain because:

> Australian society was not yet heavily industrialised, its poverty was not so widespread nor as chronic, and the climate made it less harsh. In addition, there existed no leisured class with time and money to help the less fortunate, nor well-established churches to undertake social service work.[54]

By the 1890s the charity impulse was quickening in the capital cities as pressure was put on governments, secular agencies and churches to do more for the disadvantaged. Lawrence observes, for example, that the Melbourne relief scene was busy enough by 1887 to warrant the formation of a charity organisation society:

> Three years later, it sponsored the first Australasian Conference on Charity, followed by a second in 1891. Many voluntary agencies were represented at these conferences, and a significant proportion of the delegates were women and clergymen. The scope of the conferences was broad. For instance, topics proposed for discussion at the first conference included 'principles of charity organisation', 'hospitals and treatment of the sick', 'indoor relief', 'outdoor relief', 'treatment of the dependent', and 'reformation of the criminal'. It was hoped that by establishing communication between charitably minded colonists, the conference would begin an important era in the history of Australian philanthropic effort.[55]

These forums were coliseums for the age-old clash between competing versions of disadvantage. The idea that each man or women could master their own personal destiny was strong in the colonies and it drove, as it does today, a minimalist concept of charity. People, so this Social Darwinian approach said, became destitute or sick or sad largely because of moral weakness.

The other version, which was soon to flex its muscles, developed in the shadow of a deepening economic depression, the second worst in Australia's economic history after the Great Depression of the 1930s. The end of the gold rush overlapped the start of an unprecedented ten-year drought. Bankrupt farmers, sacked farm workers, wool prices dropping by 50%, emerging trade union militancy, the army called in to break up the shearers' strikes. These were big problems and they required big solutions.

During this time, the percentage of people out of work surged to 30%. Columns of men tramped from town to town looking for jobs, with their desperate families languishing in poverty at home. The poet Banjo Paterson wrote his iconic *Waltzing Matilda* about their miserable adventures. At the 1890 and 1891 Australasian Conferences on Charity referred to above, a paper was given on the unemployed. A paradigm shift was in the air. Hitherto people out of work were rarely referred to as "unemployed". They were usually described in ways consistent with the prevailing Social Darwinism: they were bludgers, lazy, stupid, shiftless, etc. Lawrence says that this paper,

> ... was ahead of its time in claiming that the unemployed were victims of the economic system, that the 'deserving' and 'undeserving' distinction was unsound, and that all people in need should be helped.[56]

This is a paraphrase of the other version of disadvantage that I mentioned above. It was a new, powerful idea of equality for all, not punitive moral judgement for a few. It bubbled hotly in a crucible of emerging national identity, industrialisation and the beginnings of the Australian workers' movement and its political arm, the Australian Labor Party. Like the 2007 global financial crisis that shook the world's confidence in capitalism, the 1890s depression exposed the fantasy of unlimited economic progress and the failings of private philanthropy. People started to look towards the State as the only institution big enough to guarantee an adequate standard of living.

After Federation

The new Australian Constitution gave the Commonwealth Governments powers to enact old age and invalid pension legislation. In one swoop the Commonwealth inaugurated the era of social security.[57] That it did so before other countries earned it the sobriquet, the "social laboratory of the world".[58] The Commonwealth did not develop any further interest in social security until World War II.

The interwar period saw the slow growth of charities. This was shown by the inquiries undertaken by the 1925–1927 Royal Commission into Social Insurance.[59] It took a close look at the charity landscape and found a great deal of uncoordinated charitable effort that operated within the prevailing mindset which had not changed much since the days of the Elizabethan Poor Laws:

> [The charitable purpose was] the suppression of begging and the encouragement of self-help. Special investigation officers visited applicants regularly to ascertain their 'character and general circumstances'. The outdoor relief provided was usually in the form of food, fuel, clothing, bedding, financial aid, finding employment, purchasing tools for employment, starting small businesses, and arranging for a rest and change in the country – cash was seldom given. Single men were provided with food and shelter, but there was an unwillingness to assist able-bodied men. Some temporary assistance was given, however, to 'the deserving unemployed'.

The Commission had found that indoor relief consisted of benevolent asylums, eventide homes for the aged, homes for patients awaiting hospital treatment, hospices providing free shelter and food for destitute men, refuges for women in distress, industrial homes for adults, homes for the care of girls and boys, and homes for infants and young children. If any charge was made for accommodation it was small.

Many organisations were providing relief for the same class of person – sometimes in the same area of a city. Several attempts had been made to establish a central coordinating organisation in each state, but many factors had prevented cooperation between the various societies.

The funds of charitable societies were privately donated or collected from charitably disposed people, and generally were subsidised by the state governments, although some societies had remained independent of government aid. Appeals were constantly being made through the daily press for assistance in special cases of extreme distress. Most of those dispensing outdoor relief for charitable organisations were unpaid.[60]

The Royal Commission reported one year before the Great Depression. This economic and social crisis was to change everything. By 1932 over one-third of the workforce, that is 337,000 men, were unemployed. Those who still had jobs were paid only 20% of what they had been paid before the Great Depression.[61] The Great Depression exposed Australian charity. It was not prepared for the mountain of distress and disadvantage with which it was confronted. Sadly, a significant welfare development that could have made a strong contribution here was still eleven years away.

February 1943, and Australia was in deep peril. Winston Churchill, the British Prime Minister, blinked first in his standoff with Australian Prime Minister, John Curtin. In one of the great sovereign building moments for the young country, Curtin insisted that Australian troops leave the Middle East and return to protect Australia from imminent Japanese invasion. In the same month that the last troops left the Middle East, Friday 12 February 1943 to be exact, Curtin's trusted Treasurer, the very principled Ben Chifley, strode into the House of Representatives to announce a cradle to the grave welfare package that would defy all expectations.[62] The package was fired in an historically unique welfare-warfare crucible.[63] The charities, if not bypassed, were largely avoided as irrelevant once the Commonwealth finally got its act together.

This was the Australian welfare state at its first zenith. It was so comprehensive in its reach that it retarded the development of charities for a generation. By the 1970s the second and last peak of the welfare interventionist state happened during the Whitlam period.[64] By then storm clouds were gathering once again over the idea that governments had a moral obligation to secure the welfare of all their citizens. The post-World War II bi-partisan Keynesian consensus was no longer holding.[65] At the time of writing, conservative governments have been in power for twenty three of the forty-three years that have passed since Whitlam. In that time, they, and their state government analogues, as well as Labor when in power, have seriously damaged the fabric of Australian society by retracting social provision in the face of rising social need. Over time, most of the silverware was sold off. The last piece, Medibank, was only recently sold to private investors and listed on the Australian Stock Exchange in 2014 by the Abbott Government.

All this retraction has produced a twofold structural consequence. Business and big charities, for very different reasons, have been energised to enter the vacant spaces left by a retreating social policy. All this was under the ideological guidance of a framework which will be described in the next section as a fundamentally flawed paradigm.

Proof of the deliberate abandonment of Australian Governments' social obligations is in the statistics. In 2016, the Organisation for Economic Cooperation and Development (OECD) rated Australia's spending on social provision the 10th worst in its survey of GDP spending on social provision amongst member states.[66] In 2016, Australia spent 19.1% of its gross domestic product on social provision such as pensions. For comparison, the country that spent the most was France, allocating 31.5%.

Recurrent or core funding first started to disappear from government welfare agencies. Then it started to disappear from the welfare charity sector. True to the hard dictates of the market, the funding that survived harsh and regular cutbacks reappeared in purchaser-provider contracts in which welfare charities delivered specific outcomes tied to erratic government policy. This market model of charity suited business but NGO charities found it difficult, and they still do. Soon, the commercial providers began to be favoured and did not mind the gag clauses in the contracts. These gag clauses did have, according to one source,

> ... a chilling effect on [non-business charities] and NGO voices began to disappear from the airwaves and print, both because of the gag and because of self-censorship from fear of repercussions.[67]

So far, this voyage into the land of giving has noted features in the history of Australian charity which show that over time two different philosophies for dispensing charity have tussled for credibility. Since the 1970s one of these philosophies has enjoyed dominance and is the vital context for all charitable activity at present. This philosophy, conservative in nature, eschews government welfare proactivity in favour of a private, market-borne solution to social need. With that context set, the next chapter takes us right into charity's operational centre.

Chapter Two
Australian Charities: Size, Shape and Controversies

Suppose everybody cared enough, everybody shared enough, wouldn't everybody have enough?

Frank Buchman, founder of the Oxford Group, 1947. [68]

First a note on definitions. Simply put, charities are not-for-profit organisations of people who come together for a "charitable purpose".[69] In 2013, the Commonwealth Parliament recognised a legislative clarification was needed to respond to the exponential growth of charities in Australia. Unfortunately, it also recognised a need to enact a major disincentive to charities speaking out against government policy. More about this shortly. Prior to the *Charities Act 2013* (Cth) coming into operation, the meaning of charity had a simple Biblical derivation that was long embedded in the common law preamble to the *Statute of Charitable Uses 1601*.[70]

The Charities Act abandoned this Biblical definition in favour of an organisational one. Within Commonwealth law a charity is now an entity that is not-for-profit and all the entity's purposes are "charitable purposes" that are for the public benefit. Furthermore, the charity is not to be an individual, political party or government authority.[71] The Act states that there are certain purposes, which if carried out by an organisation, disqualify it from claiming to be a charity. For example, organisations that break the law or act contrary to public policy.[72]

Certain *purposes* are presumed in the Act to be in the public benefit, therefore they are "charitable purposes". These range from advancing social welfare, protecting human rights, relieving the suffering of animals, to advancing education.[73] Despite the legal tightening up of the meaning of what is a charitable organisation there is still a good deal of definitional sloppiness here. For example, universities and private schools are deemed charities and are registered with the ACNC. Yet the word "charity" does not readily come to mind in defining a university's purpose. Obviously, universities (like all the other 50,000 plus registrants) are likely only on the register for the tax deductibility of donations, particularly multimillion-dollar bequests. Yet, when research is done on the charity sector in Australia, if filters are not applied, universities are lumped with typical charities like the Salvation Army. This incongruous mixing significantly distorts research results, which is another way of saying be careful of the figures I use because they are usually based on this very porous definition of charity.

Charitable Activities

So, what do registered Australian charities do? ACNC, the charity regulator, manages the mountain of information behind this question by identifying fourteen categories of charitable effort. Figure 3 explains this, giving an example of a charity in each category.

There are a few insights that we can take away from this table. First, it is hard to pick up a clear logic here in the way charitable purposes are depicted. Take for example the categories "advancing social and public welfare" and "purposes beneficial to the general public welfare". Both are vague enough to cause confusion and represent a real threat to holding charities to account. With purposes so imprecisely presented, it becomes a real challenge to synchronise performance with purpose. The second purpose, "beneficial to the general public welfare", was deliberately included to cater for charities that, upon registration with ACNC, found no other category suitably matched their purpose.[74] With 12% of all registered charities in this omnibus category, it does look like square pegs in round holes in order to win the prize of tax-deductible donations.

Another insight we can take from the table is to note that over a third of registered charities are organised religions with the *sole or main* "charitable purpose" of maintaining and perpetuating the central faith tenets of their religions. With ACNC registration, religious organisations can pursue tax-free donations for such

Charitable Purpose	Number	%	Examples (Supplied by the author)
Advancing religion	14,890	32	Baptist Union of Australia
Advancing education	9,008	19.4	The University of Queensland
Public benevolent institutions	7,766	16.7	Smith Family
Advancing social and public welfare	6,416	13.7	Life Without Barriers
Purposes beneficial to general public welfare	5,591	12	Trustee for the Institute of Public Affairs Research Trust
Advancing health	3,496	7.5	Australian Cystic Fibrosis Trust
Advancing culture	2,430	5.2	National Gallery of Australia Foundation
Advancing the natural environment	2,430	2.2	Ecological Society of Australia
Health promotion	1,386	3?	160 Men's Sheds
Promoting reconciliation	860	1.8	ANTAR Incorporated
Promoting or protecting human rights	721	1.5	Amnesty International Australia
Advancing security or safety	615	1.3	64 Surf Lifesaving Clubs in Australia
Preventing or relieving animal suffering	565	1.2	Animals Australia
Promoting or opposing changes to laws, policy, practice	391	.08	Herbert Vere Evatt Memorial Foundation (Evatt Foundation)

Figure 3. What charities do
Source: *Australian Charities Report*, op. cit., Appendix B, Table A.13, p. 86.

things as new constructions and refurbishments.[75] Also note the strong presence of universities, schools and other organisations devoted to training. Finally, note the very small (dangerously small?) number of advocacy charities. As mentioned, the government has a real problem with advocacy charities. This issue is considered shortly.

There are approximately 600,000 not-for-profit organisations (NFPs) in Australia of which only 56,177 were registered with the ACNC in 2018.[76] Approximately 246,000 not-for-profits are endorsed by the ATO for tax concessions.[77] To make it more confusing, there are approximately 130,000 incorporated associations that are "non-charitable", not-for-profits.[78] Not-for-profit organisations and registered charities are regularly treated as interchangeable.[79] The major difference is that NFPs do not rely on donor income, nor are they exposed to the regulatory regime of the ACNC. To clarify the important distinction, Figure 4 presents new profiles on a sample of NFPs that are *not* registered charities. It is worth remembering that only about 9.5% of NFPs are registered charities, yet as Figure 4 suggests these unregistered not-for-profits also embark on worthy causes.

Organisation	**Purpose**	**Income**	**Website**
Rural Health Education Fun	Provider of TV based health education for doctors and allied health workers in rural Australia.	Grants from Commonwealth Department of Health and Aging plus sale of DVDs.	www.rhef.com.au
IBBY Australia	To give children everywhere the opportunity to have access to books with high literary and artistic standards.	Membership fees	https://ibbyaustralia.wordpress.com/about/
CORENA	CORENA provides ways for people to collectively fund new renewable energy installations.	Private contributions are used to provide interest-free loans to community organisations to pay for solar installations.	https://corenafund.org.au/
Apunipima Cape York Health Council	Apunipima provides a full range of GP, allied health and health promotion services across Cape York communities.	Government grants	http://www.apunipima.org.au/how-we-work
Community Praxis Co-Op	The co-op operates as an educational, training and consultancy agency for individuals, neighbourhoods, NGOs and government authorities.	Fees for service plus government grants	http://www.communitypraxis.org/

Organisation	Purpose	Income	Website
Foresters ANA Friendly Society	Foresters Community Finance is an ethical lender with a mission to use money for the financially excluded.	Government grants plus interest on loans	https://www.foresters.org.au/about-foresters/about-us/
Girls' Time Out	GTO Young Women's Support Service Inc provides a range of programs to homeless and at risk of homelessness young women, including parents across the Rockhampton Local Government Area.	Government grants	http://girlstimeout.com.au/
The Coalition on Criminal Assault in the Home	Townsville-based organisation that offers a safe places program for people escaping situations of homophobic violence.	Government grants	
Purple House. Western Desert Nganampa Walytja Palyantjaku Tjutaku Aboriginal Corporation	Alice Springs-based health service providing clinic-based and mobile dialysis mainly to remote Aboriginal communities.	Government and philanthropic grants.	https://www.purplehouse.org.au/the-purple-house
Great Mates Inc	Great Mates purpose is to assist young people in building their confidence and self-esteem to enable them to be a contributing member of the community.	Government grants	http://www.ourcommunity.com.au/directories/listing?id=8173

Figure 4. A sampling of not-for-profit organisations not registered as charitable organisations despite carrying out a charitable purpose.

Note. One of the data sources for this table was Australian Government, Department of Social Services, Communities and Vulnerable People, Approved Projects 2014, https://www.dss.gov.au/our-responsibilities/communities-and-vulnerable-people/approved-projects-projects-listing-by-state/territory/approved-projects-qld. Some of these organisations may no longer exist. All these organisations were checked on the ACNC register database on 9 August 2018 and none showed registered status.

Sector	Total Income ($m)	Employment
Wholesale trade	484,697	531,000
Manufacturing	378,357	838,000
Mining	179,334	163,000
Australian Charities	**152,420**	**1,355,000**
Agriculture	100,966	481,000
Information, media and telecommunications	79,909	170,000
Arts and Recreation	34,392	209,000

Figure 5. Comparison of the Charity Sector with other Sectors, 2015–16.
Source: *Australian Charities Report,* op. cit., 2016, Appendix B, Figure A.1. p. 79. This is an abridged version of the table to show where the charity sector fits with other sectors around it.

With the difference between registered and non-registered charities made, the focus now must fall on registered charities because that is where the data are. The first point to make, and a surprising one to many people, is the enormous size of the sector. In 2016, the total combined revenue of registered charities in the Australian charity sector was $152.4 billion.[80] When the charity sector is compared to other sectors (see Figure 5 above) it is clear that the registered charity sector is a very significant part of the Australian economy.

Registered Australian charities, from these figures, are an economic force to be reckoned with: smaller than mining but bigger than agriculture. The charity sector in 2016 was the largest employer with about 1.4 million workers.[81]

Size (ANC definition)	Number	%
Small (annual revenue less than $250,000)	33,941	67
Medium (annual revenue $250,000 – $999,999)	7,969	15.7
Large (annual revenue $1 million or more)	8,757	17.3
Total	50,667	100

Figure 6. Size of Registered Australian Charities 2016.
Source: *Australian Charities Report,* op. cit., 2016, Figure A.2, p. 80.

Another surprise awaits us. Most charities are quite small. One study showed that 37% of all registered charities have incomes below $50,000, with the top 20% of charities commanding a massive 95.8% of all charitable income.[82]

The ACNC has a three-way categorisation of registered charities by revenue, as Figure 6 explains.

In terms of annual revenue, registered charities sit on a ridiculously wide spectrum: from Australia's largest "charity", the University of Melbourne, with current revenue around $2.3 billion, to Australia's smallest charity, the unheard of Building Angels Ltd, with a revenue in 2016 of $10. The table below (Figure 7), using the Data.government database, shows the ten biggest charities and some of the ten smallest charities in terms of 2016 revenue.

If you take a close look at this table two anomalies will strike you. First, three Australian universities are on this list. I have

Biggest Charities	**Revenue**	**Smallest Charities**	**Revenue**
University of Melbourne	$2.35 billion	Building Angels Ltd	$10
Roman Catholic Archdiocese of Brisbane	$2.21 billion	Carry for Kids Inc	$20
University of Sydney	$2.13 billion	Remed Environmental Health Ltd	$30
Monash University	$2.08 billion	Madina Village Community Services	$40
Queensland Sugar Ltd	$1.91 billion	Water Street Occasional Care	$50
University of New South Wales	$1.89 billion	Meat for Fridays Ltd	$60
St. Vincent's Health Australia Ltd	$1.88 billion	Southland Compassion Inc	$70
The University of Queensland	$1.75 billion	Southern Cross Wellness Centre	$80
St. John of God Health Care Inc	$1.55 billion	Mental Health Matters	$90
Uniting Care Queensland	$1.43 billion	Winnejup Bushfire Brigade	$100

Figure 7. Biggest and Smallest Charities 2016.
*10,993 registered charities did not have any revenue in 2016. The ten smallest charities presented here are a sample of charities that made less than $100 revenue in 2016. Sources. For biggest charities, *Australian Charities Report,* op. cit., 2016, Appendix C, Figure A.35, p. 102. For smallest charities ACNC 2016 AIS Dataset.[415] 2016 was the last year ACNC reported on the specific revenue of large charities.

previously been critical of universities being recognised as charities, as it is nothing more than a sleight-of-hand grasp for more public funds.

The other anomaly, and the one that shows the farcical consequence of the floppy definition of what constitutes a charity, is the presence on these top ten charities list of the Queensland Sugar Ltd (QSL). QSL describes itself as "a not-for-profit, service organisation owned by Queensland cane growers and sugar millers, which is dedicated to serving their interests for the long-term prosperity of the Queensland sugar industry".[83] A strictly commercial operation, with no donors and no charity programs is recognised as a charity by the ACNC, in fact recognised as the fifth biggest charity in Australia!

Yes, hard to believe. Even harder is to understand Queensland Sugar's deformed logic in justifying why it self-nominated to be on the charity register. In its 2018 Activity Information Statement to the regulator, QSL said, in response to the regulator's question: "what charitable work did you do in 2018"? QSL replied (paraphrased), "Continued to promote the development of the Australian sugar industry through providing services to all of Queensland's growers and Millers (*sic*)".[84] So there you have it! Every time you sit down for a cuppa and put sugar in your tea or coffee, QSL is right behind you nodding approvingly that it has just performed another charitable act. With millions of cups of tea and coffee consumed daily in Australia maybe it's right that QSL is Australia's fifth largest charity.

The field is now wide open for other commercial entities to re-structure their corporate affairs in a similar way to QSL in order to achieve charitable recognition. And I do mean wide open: cigarette companies, arms dealers, toothpaste manufacturers and the like.

The final observation around this farce is that obviously the ACNC is not making *any* moral judgments on the charitable purposes that organisations claim they sponsor. I say this in light of the vigorous health debate which implicates the consumption of sugar in a range of pathologies.[85] Should moral assessment be part of any charity regulator's brief? Tantalising as it is, this question is outside the scope of the book.

Having considered the big charities, let's turn our attention to the small ones. A 2015 study showed that there were 18,892 extra-small charities registered with ACNC.[86] Thirty nine percent (7,311 charities) had incomes greater than zero but less than $10,000 per year.[87] At this scale, these charities would be highly local, offering a service into a narrow niche market. These extra-small charities usually don't have the money to employ professional staff. In 2015, extra-small charities employed a total of 26,177 staff. While this means that on average each small charity could employ 1.3 persons, we must remember that over two-thirds of these were casual staff (66.9%). But averaging does not work here as four out of five extra-small charities engaged no paid staff at all.[88] This means that extra-small charities depend on high levels of volunteerism. The Australian charity sector, in line with overseas trends, is overwhelmingly volunteer dependent. In 2015, 2.97 million volunteers were engaged in the sector, with the biggest proportion shared across the religion, social services and health parts of the sector.[89] On average, twenty-three volunteers worked in each of these small charities. Again, the spread is not even. Sixty eight percent of small charities (12,922) operated solely on voluntary engagement.

The way extra-small charities are funded also points to a tenuous existence. Government grants comprised only 5.7% of the total income of these small charities whereas among all charities income from government comprised 41.4% of income. Extra-small charities received 38% of income from donations and bequests, compared with 8.3% for all charities. These figures take us back to the points raised at the beginning of Chapter One. The current charity landscape is very much supermarkets and corner stores.

Responding to this state of affairs, one commentator says he fears a welfare arms race:

> ... in which the lion's share of government funding will go to super-sized welfare businesses, some of which will be 'for-profit' in nature, while the smaller, community-based and faith-based organisations will be marginalised or left completely undone. [90]

In a recent conference paper, Butcher has argued that gains in voice and public leverage have mainly accrued to what he calls "Big Charity".[91] This leads into a consideration of whether big charities get the lion's share of the donation dollar.

Profile of Giving

When the income sources of charities are considered there are some further surprises. Half of all charitable income comes from what researchers call “other income”. This refers to income from sale of goods, user pay arrangements, members’ fees, interest and dividends on investments, etc. Obviously, this income profile reflects the largest charities in the sector. The next income stream is government grants, accounting for 42% of the pie. Finally, there is donated income, accounting for only 8% of all charitable income.[92]

One gets a strong (if disputed) impression of the size of the Australian charity sector when this 8% individual donor income is considered. In money terms this proportion totalled $12.5 billion in 2015–16, with an average donation of $764.[93] Further insights into individual giving are provided by the National Australia Bank’s Charitable Giving Index, which monitors direct transfers into its accounts owned by charitable organisations. Year by year comparisons of this index suggest that the amount of donations follows the age profile of the Australian population with the 65 and over age group the most generous and the 15 to 24 age group the least generous.[94] The most obvious reason for the disparities in benevolence here is the variable access to disposable income. Other explanations remain as delicious research questions, such as whether the spirit of generosity is age related. The NAB Indexes also reveal a decline in generosity with the biggest decline in the 55 to 64 age group. This could be the group less resilient to strong economic headwinds such as unemployment and cost of living increases.

Assessments within the charity sector suggest that at any one time there are about 3000 people in Australia actively canvassing donations on behalf of these charities through face to face contacts and telemarketing.[95]

One of the last remaining things to do in this chapter is to pull out for closer inspection the coming showdown between charities and government over the issue of free speech.

Advocacy Charities: Not on My Watch!

In 2006, a small charity entered the cross hairs of the Howard Government. The full force of the Australian Taxation Office (ATO) was applied against Aid/Watch, a charity whose purpose was to monitor and campaign around the delivery of overseas aid.[96] Aid/Watch had been accepted by ATO as a charitable institution and as such received various taxation exemptions.[97] The ATO Commissioner revoked these exemptions in October 2006 on the grounds that he believed that Aid/Watch was a political organisation. From that point on Aid/Watch was in a hard, four-year David and Goliath legal struggle with the ATO. After the Tax Commissioner disallowed an objection to his decision, Aid/Watch appealed to the Administrative Appeals Tribunal and won. In the commonplace see-saw in appeals, the AAT found that Aid/Watch's major objective was the relief of poverty, but the Full Court of the Federal Court found that Aid/Watch's main purpose was not charitable but political. The matter was decided by the High Court in December 2010.[98] By a 5:2 majority Aid/Watch got its charitable status because the charity contributed to public welfare, end of story, for the time being.

Three years after the High Court decision in Aid/Watch, the Gillard Labor Government brought in the *Charities Act, 2013*. It is clear from the Bill's second reading that the government was positively influenced by the Aid/Watch decision. Lindsay Bradbury, then Assistant Treasurer and Minister Assisting for Deregulation, said:

> The bill reflects the Aid/Watch decision that charities may have a purpose to generate public debate about a charitable purpose. It allows for an entity to have a charitable purpose, including a sole purpose, of promoting or opposing a change in the law or government policy relevant to another charitable purpose.[99]

The Explanatory Memorandum to the Charities Bill made it clear what political action charities can involve themselves in without risking deregistration: "Charities are not prevented ... from distributing information, critiquing or comparing party policies in order to further the achievement of their charitable purpose".[100]

Johns appears not to have read this part of the Explanatory Memorandum. His response to the High Court decision in the Aid/Watch decision was predictable, if not a little worrying:

> The Abbott government promised to abolish the Charities Act 2013, which includes advocacy as a charitable purpose. It must

make good that promise in a way that makes it clear to the High Court that advocacy is not a charitable purpose.[101]

While this High Court decision will impact on any future deregistration efforts by ACNC (see the Catholic Education Melbourne matter below) it is obvious that the charity advocacy hunting season has opened.

How times have changed! The acceptance of the advocacy role was set out back in a 1991 statement by the House of Representatives Standing Committee on Community Affairs:

> An integral part of the consultative and lobbying role of these organisations is to disagree with government policy where this is necessary in order to represent the interests of their constituencies.[102]

Twenty-three years later and we are in a new hard game. Johns' book, *The Charity Ball*, (see page 77), was his application in the prevailing social and political mood in Canberra for the ACNC job. He argued that the government should remove advocacy as a charitable purpose. He cited as a case in point the Queensland Environmental Defenders Office, much hated by the conservative side of politics because it is against coal mining, even though it is not a registered charity.[103] He also criticised big charities "whose service delivery is heavily weighted towards advocacy, research, campaigning and lobbying".[104] We can use this as context when we examine below the ACNC's first strike against a so-called advocacy charity, Catholic Education Melbourne:

> **SENATOR KETTER** [ALP Queensland]: Under the Charities Act charities are precluded under threat of losing their charitable status from pursuing a political purpose, which you've mentioned. Do you think the definition of political purpose in the Charities Act is clear and well understood by the charities?
> **DR JOHNS** [ACNC Chair]: ... it seems to me to be clear enough that unless it's an explicit advocacy for or against a political party or candidate then you're free to say and do whatever. It gets a little bit unclear when you've said everything but 'vote for that party' but we don't have a case that easily defines that.[105]

Johns believes he may have that case now. On request, the ACNC received an extra $1 million in the 2018 Budget to fund any test case the regulator may have to respond to if or when a charity loses its registration for engaging in advocacy.[106]

On 19 July 2018 three Australian Catholic Archbishops met with the then Prime Minister, Malcolm Turnbull to voice their concern at the recent action by ACNC to investigate whether Catholic Education Melbourne should be deregistered.[107]

A week before the Batman by-election on 17 March 2018, Catholic Education Melbourne distributed leaflets and put through over 30,000 robocalls to electors.[108] The purpose of the action was to ask voters not to vote for the popular Greens candidate but to vote for the star Labor candidate, Ged Kearney, and thereby send a strong protest vote to Canberra about the government's school funding policy. There is no doubt that this activism helped the Labor candidate win Batman.

The ACNC bided its time and finally swooped in early July 2018. The ACNC Chair, Gary Johns, said:

> We are undertaking this investigation [of Catholic Education Melbourne] because of the activities and statements made on behalf of this one charity during the recent by-election for the federal seat of Batman. The investigation is an inquiry about the activities and purposes of the charity. It has arisen from a concern that the charity may have a disqualifying purpose and therefore may not be entitled to be a registered charity.[109]

Under the *Charities Act* if an organisation has a "disqualifying purpose" then it cannot be registered, or, as in the present case, can have its registration revoked. There are two "disqualifying purposes":

— engaging in, or promoting, activities that are unlawful or contrary to public policy, and
— promoting or opposing a political party or candidate for political office.

The ACNC is attempting to skewer Catholic Education Melbourne on either or both these hooks. In the first instance, Catholic Education Melbourne stands to be deregistered because its activism during the Batman by-election was contrary to government policy. In the second instance, Catholic Education Melbourne stands to be deregistered because it supported the

Labor candidate in order to send a message to Canberra about its controversial school funding policy. On these grounds Catholic Education Melbourne could be in trouble.

But then again, they might be OK because the ACNC falls into hopeless contradiction around how to interpret its own statutory framework. On its website the ACNC advises:

> A charity can promote or oppose a change to any matter of law, policy or practice in furtherance or aid of *another charitable purpose*. The law, policy or practice being promoted or opposed can be anywhere in Australia or overseas (emphasis added).

So far, so good for Catholic Education Melbourne. It is registered with ACNC as having the charitable purpose of "advancing education". It would be a bizarre argument to conclude that the purpose of Catholic Education Melbourne's Batman by-election advocacy was not related to its charitable purpose. The ACNC statement continues:

> The public benefit of advocacy is its contribution to public discussion, which informs the public and policy makers. The methods of advocacy used, and its aims must not be inconsistent with the rule of law and the established system of government.[110]

I'm not sure what advocacy inconsistent with the established system of government would look like, but there is no evidence that Catholic Education Melbourne broke any laws during that campaign. The ACNC has certainly had to wear a lot of excoriation over its action, including a sharply worded editorial in *The Australian*.[111]

It will be interesting to see how Johns' and the Institute of Public Affairs (IPA) case against charity advocacy pans out. The answer might just be hidden in two recommendations from a recent review of the *Charities Act* and the ACNC:

> **Chapter 9 – Advocacy**
> 19. The ACNC be resourced to enable the Commissioner to enforce and develop the law where registered entities engage in disqualifying purposes.
> 20. Test case funding be made available to develop the law in matters of public interest, including disqualifying purposes.[112]

If the government accepts these recommendations, and there is every likelihood it will, then Johns will get a war chest to nullify the High Court in Aid/Watch. The trigger could be the threatened de-registration of Catholic Education Melbourne.

The present move against Catholic Education Melbourne is significant because it's the first evidence we have of the resolve to rein in charities that criticise government action. The medium to large charities can expect more exposure to this censorship as they possess the resources to hurt governments in any fight back action. The threatened de-registration of Catholic Education Melbourne is also significant because it shows a clear double standard. It seems that there are advocacy charities that the government likes and advocacy charities that it doesn't like.

Three examples come to mind illustrating this hypocrisy. In the March 2017 Western Australian election, the registered charity, the Australian Christian Lobby, handed out political leaflets in targeted polling booths urging electors not to vote for the Australian Labor Party candidate because of their support for the controversial Safe Schools Program.[113] This is exactly what Catholic Education Melbourne is accused of but there is no evidence of the ACNC investigating the Australian Christian Lobby.

The second example concerns the registered charity, the Institute of Public Affairs (IPA). This gets a little interesting because, as mentioned earlier, the current Chair of ACNC, Gary Johns, was once a senior research fellow at the IPA. On any fair assessment, the IPA must rank as the advocacy charity *par excellence* in Australia today. The IPA is Australia's foremost right wing think tank. It has, since its inception in 1943 (ironically the same year the National Welfare Scheme was announced), been the ideological powerhouse for a minimalist approach to government, and more pertinent here, a minimalist approach to government welfare spending. It also harbours more climate denialists than in Donald Trump's executive team. With its impeccable connections to the Australian Liberal Party, big business and the Murdoch media, it is indeed a force to be reckoned with.

The IPA has a secret and 'indirect' approach to its funding sources. It never says who its donors are and has made statements of dubious veracity to the charity regulator, the Australian Charities and Not-for-profits Commission, about these donations.

In the year to 30 June 2016 it claimed to have received $529,804 from donors. It failed to mention to the regulator that in the same period it received $2.3 million from Australia's richest woman and celebrity climate denier, Gina Rinehart. In the following year, the IPA told the regulator that it received $627,060 in donations. Again, it failed to record a $2.2 million donation from Rinehart to the regulator.[114]

With this secret donation funding, the IPA frequently storms the media with anti-welfare invective. It has, it says:

> ... been at the forefront of the political and policy debate, defining the contemporary political landscape ... The IPA supports ... the free flow of capital, [and] a limited and efficient government ...[115]

It has "been at the forefront of the political and policy debate", yet the IPA is registered with ACNC under the category, "Purposes beneficial to the general public welfare". What is the IPA up to that it does not want to be seen in the category, "Promoting or opposing a change to laws, policy or practice"? This, despite a warning from ACNC that, "If all of your charity's purposes fall within other subtypes, do not select this subtype".[116] Could it be the IPA fears a fate now possibly awaiting Catholic Education Melbourne?

The IPA's rightful category for charitable purposes is surely: "Promoting or opposing a change to laws, policy or practice", a category cheerfully ticked by its left-wing counterpart, the Evatt Foundation.[117] What category an organisation ends up in is usually determined by the charities themselves with minimal vetting by ACNC.[118] Vetting the authenticity of claims made by charities as to what their true purposes are remains a significant challenge for the ACNC. This brings risk into the ACNC's regulatory operations because it is possible that organisations are not what they seem.

Finally, there was the Israel Folau controversy that shook the headlines in 2019. The relevant point here is that the powerful religious pressure group, the Australian Christian Lobby (ACL), raised over $1.8 million towards an astounding $3 million target for Folau's legal war chest to fight his dismissal from the Australian Rugby Union Wallaby's team on religious freedom grounds. The Australian Charities and Not-for-profits Commission has refused to say how many complaints it has received from people questioning whether the ACL is in breach of its charitable purpose.[119] It will be interesting to see whether the regulator mounts a formal investigation or drops the matter, like it did with the complaint against ACL for alleged political interference in the 2017 Western Australian election (see above).

The advocacy controversy is simply part of a deeper conflict. How human society has responded to social need is as timeless as the polarised answers the question summons. The history of charity is really an account of this timelessness. Nothing seems to change. Maybe "history" is the wrong word then. What we have, it appears, is a permanent, polarised, ideological struggle around two questions: "what is social need?" and "how to respond to it?" For want of a better description, the struggle is between one ideological camp that flies under the "more government-less charities" banner versus the other ideological camp that musters under the "less government-more charities" flag. At any one time, from the colonial period to now, one of the polarised positions is ascendant. Right now, the position that says social need is personal and should be responded to privately has taken over the administration of charitable action. It is an uneasy ascendancy and the future cannot predict for how long this framework will maintain credit. What we do know is that we are in the golden age of (business) charities, and there is so much wrong with that.

Charity and Business: A Fundamentally Flawed Paradigm

In a speech on the future of the community welfare sector on 27 May 2014 Tony Nicholson, then CEO of the highly respected Melbourne charity, the Brotherhood of St. Laurence, said:

> Our sector has evolved to a critical stage underpinned by a particular paradigm. Central to this paradigm is the idea that our sector can continue to meet society's current and emerging needs by contracting to government, expanding and aggregating organisations, driving for greater efficiency, and further professionalising, regulating and circumscribing care. To my mind it is a paradigm that is fundamentally flawed. I sense it is sapping the very ethos and moral drive of the sector and, with it, the wider community. While it may have served us reasonably well over the last 30 years — driving the improvement in the

> quality, scope and reach of services — it cannot take us into the next 30.[120]

Strong words and acute observations. The paradigm that Nicholson refers to usually goes under the name government, clueless academics and shallow-thinking social commentators gave it when it first emerged with gusto in the 1970s. The name is "neo-liberalism" aka "economic rationalism". There is nothing "neo" or indeed "liberal" or indeed "rational" about a paradigm that licences governments to turn their core welfare responsibilities over to the profit mania of business. No, let's call it for what it is: welfare capitalism, with all the greed, near-sightedness and crass opportunism that is usually associated with this label.

Nicholson's thoughtful talk is less a speech and more a denunciation of future dystopian possibilities. This is his take on the future if welfare capitalism is not neutralised:

> The prevailing paradigm of gathering paid professional people around the vulnerable in our community will become unviable in the next twenty years. At least two factors are at play — workforce and funding. First, the workforce question. As our population ages, and the proportion of people of workforce age declines, we have to ask where are the workers going to be found? Competition for skilled labour will become fierce.[121]

Starved of professional staff who will have better prospects in the for-profit sector, Nicholson foresees a reversion back to "... more Dickensian models of care we joyously left behind in the 1980s, or even collapse".[122]

Nicholson could see in his dystopian vision a drying up of the voluntary spirit that has bed-rocked charities in Australia since colonial times:

> We [will] not only lose the sense of responsibility that citizens have for issues in their community ... we [will] also lose the diversity of networks and connections and opportunities that the broader community can bring to social needs. And most importantly we lose that intangible quality of authenticity that is created through voluntary caring relationships. As a consequence, the richness and effectiveness of service provision is greatly reduced.[123]

The message is that there is one thing called care and compassion and there is another thing called business. Disciples of the current charity-business paradigm assume that when these two things intermingle, only positive outcomes can occur.[124]

As the following three vignettes so clearly show, when business and charity get together, business can so completely dominate the agenda that the charitable outcomes are seriously compromised.[125] The first vignette shows what happens to a well-regarded charity when a new chairman with very strong capitalist values comes on board. The second case details what happens when a multinational health and welfare provider sinks its wealth into a chain of nursing homes and profits by giving seriously degraded services. The final vignette illustrates the appalling anti-social behaviour business is capable of when its profits are threatened in administering a charity.

Save the Children or Save the Dollar

Sir Alan Parker has been the chair of Save the Children UK since 2008. Previously, Parker, with a personal fortune of £150 million, was the head of the Brunswick Group, a PR firm with mega rich connections. In fact, the company has a third of the FTSE 100 top firms as clients. The British Broadcasting Corporation (BBC) ran a story in March 2018 alleging that Parker and Save the Children UK as a whole had mishandled complaints of sexual harassment and bullying lodged against some of the charity's senior managers.[126] A petition was soon circulating among staff demanding Parker's resignation, and the British Government's Charities Commission announced they would run an inquiry into the organization. A week after the inquiry was announced, Parker resigned.

According to a report in the *Non-Profit Quarterly*:

> Current and former employees say the charity, under the leadership of Parker, created an adrenalized culture more suited to a battle-ready business than a charity. They describe a place gripped by a desire to win, with victory defined as raising more money and then spending it on splashier projects than other charities did. There were boasts about reaching more children. Dollars and headlines were key metrics. Beating Oxfam, a UK-based charity that fights poverty, was the goal.[127]

Parker "was putting growth above all", said Jonathan Glennie, former director of policy and research (at Save the Children UK) "and the cost was that anything that got in the way of growth was ignored".[128]

Parker's strategy was to position Save the Children UK as a massive donor-taking machine. As one commentator close to the action said:

> As Save the Children UK started to act more like a corporation, it raised more money from publicly traded companies. Within three years of Mr. Parker's appointment, business sponsorships had quintupled to nearly $30 million—even if some of those deals appeared too close for comfort. Communications staff were sometimes asked, according to this report, to delay issuing critiques of companies that were donors or prospective donors.

This happened a few times when the press office wanted to chastise energy companies, including British Gas and EDF, for raising rates, said Dominic Nutt, the charity's one-time head of news. "If the money got in the way of the mission," he said in an interview, "the money came first."[129]

In the end, Parker left Save the Children UK with serious damage to its reputation and as always follows, a reduction in donations.

Save the Children UK remains a troubled organisation. The short answer as to why this is so is embedded in the flawed charity-business paradigm that dominates the current welfare narrative.

Business people on the charity boards, come Trojan-like, armed with spread sheets, calculators and tax rulings. Business people (even those with the best of intentions) will solve welfare and health problems the business way, not the welfare way. For example, client participation in management is heresy in the business model. Of the current sixteen members of the Board of Trustees of Save the Children UK, ten come from high level business backgrounds.[130] So it is not surprising that Save the Children UK seems to be in a rolling crisis management pattern, forever dealing with the contradictions that suppurate out of the charity-business paradigm. Their latest crisis occurred on 21 December 2018. Save the Children UK lost its Chair when Peter

Bennett-Jones was pushed out for making comments to staff that could be seen as, "being at odds with the charity's review of its working culture" instigated after the resignation of Sir Alan Parker.[131] Unquestionably, the crisis Save the Children UK finds itself in as the business model is imposed on the charity model will not spare Australian charities.

Bupa: Big Business, Small Care

Such is the case, as I write, with the Royal Commission into Aged Care Quality and Safety. The more than six thousand submissions received by the Commission since it started in October 2018 tell horrific tales of elder abuse and neglect. The Bupa Group came in for hostile criticism during evidence to the Royal Commission. Bupa has six thousand elderly men and women in seventy-two nursing homes in Australia. Of these:

- 45 have failed to meet all the health and safety standards
- 22 homes have been declared as putting the health and safety of residents at "serious risk"
- 13 Bupa homes have been sanctioned, which means they have lost government funding and are unable to take new residents
- 4 other homes — NSW's Berry and Eden, Victoria's Traralgon and Tasmania's South Hobart — have had their accreditation revoked and then re-accredited.[132]

In an interview with *The 7.30 Report's* Leigh Sales, on 11 September 2019, Bupa's CEO, Hisham El-Ansary, apologised for the failures of care exposed on the program, saying they were "totally unacceptable". El-Ansary said:

> It's evident that there was a period there where we lost our focus on what we were doing, and I can tell you that since coming into the role earlier this year it has been my number one priority to put in place those mechanisms and new teams and new people to address these issues.

The discerning viewer was perfectly entitled to throw beer cans at the TV screen when El-Ansary made these comments. El-Ansary's no doubt genuine message from the heart has to be seen with the message from his head which is clearly processing the reputational costs to a large healthcare multinational if the elder abuse and neglect suffered by vulnerable Australians in his nursing homes is not stopped. El-Ansary was hardly being creative in his response to Leigh Sales' searching observations. His was the old two-punch manoeuvre: "I am sorry", quickly followed by, "I am new, the team's new, and we are back on track".

The scandal around the maladministration of Bupa's nursing homes broke on 12 September 2019.[133] Right on time, just four days later, Bupa took shelter from the gathering storm clouds by announcing a quick fix that was embarrassingly shallow and clearly disingenuous.

On 16 September, Bupa's aged care managing director, Suzanne Dvorak, promised she would make surprise visits to some of the company's embattled residential centres alongside a public advocate, to "find out the truth" of what was happening.[134] What nonsense! Research has shown that these strategies offer nil guarantee of future performance of scandal-ridden organisations.[135]

Who then is the Bupa Group? The company itself tells us that it has thirty-two million customers in one hundred and ninety countries. It looks after twenty-two thousand aged care residents and it "... re-invests profits to help our members live longer, healthier and happier lives".[136] It also tells us that it is heavily into the mergers and acquisitions strategy. That is why it moved to Australia in 2011, having acquired three long-running private health insurers: MBF, HBA and Mutual Community.

Since its move to Australia, Bupa has sailed in and out of scandals. It was announced in March 2019 that Bupa Australia will pay $157 million to the Australian Taxation Office after reaching an in-principle deal following an investigation into the company that involved claims of tax dodging.[137] Psychologists treating military personnel claim they are out of pocket tens of thousands of dollars since Bupa took over the Commonwealth Defence health contract in July, and have warned that a logjam with referrals could be putting lives at risk. A Sydney psychologist said Bupa has failed to pay up on two hundred and seventy invoices worth an estimated $73,000 over a nine-week period.[138]

The Australian (and New Zealand) market has been very good to the Bupa Group. In fact, it derives more growth and profit from these markets than from the other countries in its worldwide reach. In the first half of 2019, the Bupa Group had revenue in these specific markets to the tune of $4.5 billion and $142 million profit (up 37%).[139] Here is the flawed business-charity model *in extremis*. It congregates power and profits and disperses risk, quality and accountability. So large and complicated is the conglomerate that its owners in 1 Angel Court, London probably won't need to be bothered reading the final recommendations of the Royal Commission into Aged Care Quality and Safety.

We are getting good evidence now that large multinationals in the health and welfare areas are persistently change-resistant. Bupa, Vatican style, keeps for itself at 1 Angel Place, London, the big questions such as: "shall we sell our nursing home assets and become an arms importer?" and gives paltry autonomy to local units around little questions such as: "what colour shall we paint the day room?" So, we can predict some local adjustments to whatever recommendations come out of the aforementioned Royal Commission, but major opposition in the unlikely event the Royal Commission brings down hard recommendations that impact on Bupa profit.

The Earle Haven Retirement Village Scandal

Finally, we examine the recent scandal at a Brisbane nursing home that truly exposes the dark heart of the business paradigm.

> **Welcome to Earle Haven Retirement Village**
> **The best resort style way of life on the Gold Coast.**
>
> Nestled between the golden beaches and the lush Hinterland, Earle Haven, the "Garden Paradise" has been the first choice of retirees for over two decades. Situated on Queensland's fabulous Gold Coast, Earle Haven offers resort style living combined with a comprehensive range of Government funded, residential Aged Care facilities.
>
> A selection of one, two- and three-bedroom independent living units are available within 4G acres of award winning, tropical gardens. Also available are one bedroom or studio style, serviced apartments within the "Lodge".
>
> Our residents enjoy an extensive range of on-site activities and amenities and easy access to surrounding shopping centres

> such as Surfers Paradise, Pacific Fair and Helensvale Westfield. Also, within walking distance are three local centres. Residents also enjoy the use of our courtesy bus, covered heated pool, fully licensed, a la carte restaurant and dining room, coffee shop and club house. Close by is Carrara Stadium, regularly hosting a range of sporting and other events.
>
> All this with the added security of CCT monitored streets and 24 hour on-site emergency care staff.[140]

Fast forward from this beguiling version of paradise to the afternoon of 11 July 2019 and we have developing at Earle Haven Retirement Village an event so shocking that it exposes the true dark heart of the government's favourite model for welfare and health service.[141]

> There was a couple of residents as I [ambulance officer] entered the foyer area, reception area. There was a gentleman in a wheelchair who was being looked after. His urinary bag was being dragged as he was trying to push himself to the foyer. That was in the middle of an argument between a number of staff. And there was an elderly tall gentleman who became very disoriented, became what you'd call – if you didn't know dementia, would be seen to be aggressive, raising his voice, raising his hands, very emotional about what's happening around him ...
>
> There was one elderly lady that I was asked to intervene and provide care to, just outside the reception area. She was approximately-92-year-old female, very distressed, very disorientated, crying. Her daughter was there; she was crying as well, trying to get the elderly lady to settle down and comfort her, and she just kept crying and screaming that – she thought her daughter was her mother and kept referring to her as her mother, to – "Please stop this." She was later taken back into the foyer area. She was assessed by the senior medical officer and also the residential doctor who had come in to assist us. She was then deemed not safe to be transported to another nursing facility so, therefore, was transported through to a public hospital.[142]
>
> A 92-year-old woman with dementia was crying and screaming, asking her "mother" to stop the chaos as distressed aged care residents were evacuated from their Queensland home. ...

One staff member had to be surrounded by police officers after other staff threatened to "punch her head in" if she did not give them patient care folders.[143]

Gold Coast Health executive Karlene Willcocks said that one of the residents she spoke to that day told her he realised the home was in trouble when a blanket was whipped off him as he lay in bed. She was there as part of the "mass casualty action plan" that responded to the confusing closure of the facility, as fridges, mops, buckets and even kitchen equipment were wheeled out. Even items like disposable rubber gloves had been taken.[144]

This is the charity-business model in full heartless swing. That afternoon, high-care residents of Earle Haven Retirement Village were summarily evicted, there is no other word for it. Because of what? A fire risk, a food poisoning issue, an outbreak of disease? No, because of a contract dispute between the owner and the organisation that ran the facility. This extraordinary event has many shadows over it. My purpose is to provide a brief reckoning of the human costs when greed meets care. The situation at Earle Haven has been referred to the Royal Commission and it is possible the owner will face adverse findings when the Commission makes its final report.

The approved provider of the Earle Haven Retirement Village is People Care Pty Ltd, the principal of which is Arthur Miller. Since at least March 2018, an entity called HelpStreet associated with Hong Kong based Kristopher Bunker, has been managing the facility under an arrangement with People Care. The cessation of services on 11 July 2018 appears to have been the result of a dispute between People Care and HelpStreet. It resulted in a 000 callout to the Queensland Ambulance Service which took charge of the care of residents and, throughout the remainder of the day, on the 11th and the early hours of the 12th, transported the residents to other nursing-homes and hospitals. This was, understandably, distressing for both residents and their families.[145]

From its approval in 2006 as a provider of community, flexible and residential care, People Care appears to have had a poor compliance record, raising potential red flags about governance and management capacity. In 2015, People Care had its three-year default accreditation cycle upgraded to quite intense regulatory scrutiny by both the regulator (Aged Care Quality and Safety Commission) and the Commonwealth Department of Health.[146]

The department and the agency monitored People Care quite closely in 2016 and 2017. Their strategy was to manage Arthur Miller and his People Care into compliance with quality standards. Observations were made to the Royal Commission that Miller showed poor levels of engagement and co-operation with these processes, including in dealing with complaints. Further sanctions were imposed.[147]

As part of this monitoring, People Care was required to lodge prudential and financial statements with the Commonwealth Health Department annually. These showed that the residential-care business appeared to owe significant amounts to related companies, leaving the residential-care business, viewed in isolation, in a loss-making position and bearing heavy net liabilities.[148]

Relations between People Care and HelpStreet deteriorated in early 2019 to the point that Miller and People Care gave notice to HelpStreet that it was revoking the licence to occupy the premises on Friday, 9 August 2019.

This set the cat among the pigeons. By 11 July it appears that HelpStreet was (illegally?) removing computer equipment, metal trolleys, chairs, hygiene items and furniture from the facilities at Earle Haven. This shameless asset stripping was so robust that the emergency workers deemed the former residents were unsafe to remain at the facility and they would be better off being relocated.[149]

Telicia Tuccori was the senior clinical person at Earle Haven. This is part of her evidence before the Royal Commission:

> **Royal Commission** (henceforth **RC**): You had a serious responsibility to all of the residents ...
> **MS TUCCORI:** Yes, I did.
> **RC:** So, it was your decision ... to call the 000?
> **MS TUCCORI:** At 2 o'clock, it became apparent that, especially with the [small] amount of staff there, that something needed to happen and I did have a discussion with Karen to, I suppose, reassure myself that my decision to call 000 was correct.
> **RC:** Well, the prospect of HelpStreet leaving the facility was first raised with you on the evening of the 10th; correct?

MS TUCCORI: Correct.
RC: You appreciated, didn't you, that that meant that there would be no HelpStreet staff there to care for 70-odd residents?
MS TUCCORI: That there was a possibility, yes.
RC: Did the magnitude of that prospect mean anything to you?
MS TUCCORI: It was quite panicky. I was sort of hoping it was just a possibility and it wasn't going to come to that, but yes.
RC: Well, in your statement [you said] ... 10 July I received a phone call from Ms Parsons [executive director of HelpStreet] stating Mr Miller owed HelpStreet a large sum of money and that we were out, either tomorrow, 11 July, after 12 pm or 9 August 2019 ... Then you say that the following day it occurred to you that it might be a good idea to contact some place where respite services were available. Did you give any thought to contacting anyone on the 9th or the 10th?
MS TUCCORI: I was at a family function and wasn't really able to. Nor was I certain of the severity, I suppose you could say, or the possibilities of it being the 12th. I suppose you could call it personal opinion. I would think it would be less likely that that was going to happen because, to me, it seemed quite extreme.[150]

The Royal Commission also examined Kristopher Bunker, the Hong Kong based owner of HelpStreet. Under questioning Bunker acknowledged that he was disqualified from managing corporations under section 206F(3) of the *Corporations Act* in June 2018 for a period of three years. He said in evidence that Miller knew he was disqualified and still offered HelpStreet the management contract. He also acknowledged that the contract dispute with the Earle Haven owner was over a debt of $2.7 million plus GST that Bunker claimed Miller owed him.

Bunker had to answer some awkward questions about removing the computers which contained all the patient records including patient plan records.

RC: Finally, Mr Bunker, the servers which contained the patient records were taken from the facility on 10 July; do you recall that?
BUNKER: Yes.
RC: That was at your direction ... Well, who made the decision?
BUNKER: I was involved in it. Our management team decided that that was the best course of action.
RC: Well, why was it a good course of action?

BUNKER: To upgrade the server to a secure location.
RC: Well, did you return the server at any stage? ...
BUNKER: No.
RC: The patient records, where are they now?
BUNKER: They're on the server.
RC: Have they been provided to the providers who now have the care of these residents?
BUNKER: To the best of my knowledge, the server information has been provided.
RC: And how and when did that happen?
BUNKER: To the best of my knowledge, that's a remote access. Again, to the best of my knowledge, this is also available onsite.
RC: How is it available onsite?
BUNKER: I was assured that there was clinical hard copies onsite of care plans and documentation for resident care.
RC: Well, I'm not talking about the hard copies. I'm talking about the server and the material, the electronic information that's stored on the server. No one has got access to that, have they, except whoever has got the server; correct?
BUNKER: No, I – no, I'm of the understanding that there is remote access available to that server.
RC: All right. And where do you get that understanding from?
BUNKER: From our lawyers.
MR BOLSTER: From your lawyers? Okay.
BUNKER: Yes, correct.[151]

The tour through the world of giving is about to take a new route. The historical features of Australian charity, along with its current dimensions and controversies, have been visited and are now behind us. The next feature to explore contains darker themes.

Chapter Three
Charity Fraud and its Regulation

There is enough in the world for everyone's need, but not enough for everyone's greed.

Robert Buchanan, 1947

This chapter sets the scene for the case studies that follow. Charity fraud is a special kind of fraud. It sits away from stealing from a business. For the charity fraudster to be effective there must exist a clear and criminal intention to exploit the good intentions of the donor and thereby display a sociopathic indifference to the needy who won't get the charitable services because the money to fund them was stolen by the fraudsters. This makes charity fraud that much more insidious. Its psychological consequences can be far-reaching. The donor stung in a charity fraud may abandon further acts of charity and may even embrace a future negative view of human nature.

After considering the profile of charity fraud generally, this chapter looks at the charity regulators, particularly the relatively new boy in town, the Australian Charities and Not-for-profits Commission.

The Profile of Charity Fraud

A recent paper by the giant American accountancy firm, Baker Tilly, focused on the specific vulnerabilities of charities to fraud.[152] Unlike bureaucracies and business entities, charities tend to be encapsulated by the values and behaviours of powerful individuals, whether they be the founders, the current CEO or large donors. With ethical people in these roles there is no problem. When these roles are contaminated by crooks then there is a problem. Some of the charity fraud cases profiled further on in the book show that when leadership lapses, morally speaking, then charities can deteriorate very quickly. Two charities, the Immigrant Women's Health Service and the Non-English Speaking Housing Women's Scheme (NESH), both profiled below, took the full force of fraudulent behaviour of their CEO and had to cease functioning.

There is also a vulnerability by the nature of those people who staff the charity, whether they be paid or voluntary. These people come together out of a deep commitment to serve. Little wonder that with this focus on core missions, crucial areas such as financial oversight, budget control and auditing are overlooked, or better put, made the sole province of the powerful CEO or founder.

Furthermore, charity staff, particularly volunteers, tend to be untrained in crucial matters such as board governance and financial accountability. The very nature of charitable transactions leaves them susceptible to fraud as well. Transactions tend to be non-reciprocal, such as charitable contributions, which are easier to steal than other sources of revenue where consideration is exchanged. Additionally, charities are highly exposed to negative publicity, which can dry up donor sources overnight.

In a community with good reason to be cynical about government practice, one authority stands out, the Australian Competition and Consumer Commission (ACCC). It is accepted by a jaded community as genuinely looking after their consumer interests. Among its briefs is a requirement to protect consumers against unfair trade practices.[153] One of its programs is Scamwatch. This is an online fraud reporting service that compiles statistics from victims (or near victims) of shady operators in a range of fields such as dating, investment and, more pertinently to this study, charities.

The data it collects on charity scams makes one gasp at the level of venal criminality displayed by crooks in our community who target people of goodwill. As a subscript to this one must wonder at the level of naivety of those targeted.

Scamwatch reported that in 2017 giving Australians lost $313,280 to rogue charity operators.[154] In 2018 the figure was $211,165. That's over half a million dollars taken by charity scammers in the last two years. There is evidence that this type of scamming is on the rise because in the first four months of 2019 more money was scammed out of charity donors than for the whole of 2018.

BDO Australia, a national accountancy practice, has, until recently, administered small sample surveys monitoring the charity fraud landscape. Their 2014 survey of four hundred and thirty six respondents in Australia and New Zealand show some interesting, but tentatively placed observations:

- Fraud totalling $3,229,400 was reported, with the average fraud being $22,904.
- 55% of respondents have a code of conduct while 18% have a fraud control plan.
- The typical fraudster was aged over 50 and was a paid employee in a non-accounting role.
- Collusion was present in 30% of the largest frauds reported, with a board member involved in 31% of cases.
- Of the largest frauds reported, the most common fraud suffered by respondents was cash theft.
- 54% of respondents do not report fraud to police because of concerns relating to the impact of future funding opportunities and damage to the organisation's reputation.[155]

This of course is small change compared to the dimension of charity fraud in the USA. Baker Tilly, which has special interests in charity fraud, estimate that $US77 billion in charity fraud occurs each year across the 1.1 million not-for-profit organisations in the USA.[156] Baker Tilly lists the common charity frauds:

- Skimming — Cash is stolen before the funds are recorded in the accounting records.
- Credit card abuse — Perpetrators either use organization-issued credit cards for personal use or use donor credit card numbers.
- Fictitious vendor schemes — Perpetrators set up a company and submit fake invoices for payment.
- Conflicts of interest — Board members or executives have hidden financial interests in vendors.
- Payroll schemes — Continued payment to terminated employees, overstatement of hours, or fictitious expenditure reimbursement.

- Sub-recipient fraud — Abuses by a sub-recipient entity include intentional charges of unallowable costs to the award, fraudulent reporting of levels of effort, and reporting inaccurate performance statistics and data.
- Deceptive fundraising practices.
- Misrepresentation of the extent of a charitable contribution deduction entitlement, misrepresentation of the fair market value of donated assets, and failing to comply with donor-imposed restrictions on a gift.
- Fraudulent financial reporting.
- Misclassifying restricted donations to mislead donors or charity watchdogs, misclassifying fundraising and administrative expenses to mislead donors regarding funds used for programs, and fraudulent statements of compliance requirements with funding sources.[157]

While the focus of this book remains on the illegal and unethical practices within charities, it would be remiss not to extend the discussion briefly into the area of how charities are funded in the first place, because the way charities receive donations has triggered as much community concern as to what charities do with the money once it is in their pockets.

In an attempt to address community concerns about donation practices, and to keep more hard-hitting government regulation at bay, the big charities such as Australian Red Cross, Peter MacCallum Cancer Foundation, Plan International and the Fred Hollows Foundation have recently got together to form the Public Fundraising Regulatory Association (PFRA). This Association has established "standards" of donation-eliciting behaviour. With just over 70 charity members, it currently represents only .1% of the registered charity industry. But we are talking about the big charities here. The way they seek donations is coming more and more to our attention.

A new term has entered the English lexicon, "chuggers', charity workers on commission for the big charities who "mug" potential donors at public sites such as railway stations. The PFRA estimates that chuggers raised over $120 million and signed up 320,000 donors in 2018.[158] Chuggers work for companies which contract with the big charities. In 2018, calculations collected over five years by the PFRA found that one charity received a return of $3.30 for every dollar it invested in this kind of fundraising: the $1 cost to the charity of paying fundraisers realised $3.30 in street donations.[159] I treat that as a highly suspect figure. A Fairfax Media investigation in 2013 showed that some of Australia's biggest charities are spending almost half their donations on fundraising.[160] While the figures are a bit old, the Make-A-Wish Foundation of Australia received more than $12.8 million in donations in 2012 but spent $5.2 million, or 41¢ in the dollar, on fundraising, marketing and communications. After other expenses, only 54¢ in the donated dollar went to granting the wishes of sick children.[161] How much the collection companies charge the big charities is a well-guarded secret.[162]

In response to concerns about the standover tactics of some chuggers the Public Fundraising Regulatory Association recently announced "rules" of conduct between collectors and potential donors that they expect their member organisations to follow, such as: not initiating physical contacts, not following people and not approaching people who are seated. Four collections agencies recently had their membership of Public Fundraising Regulatory Association terminated for breaking these rules. These four agencies: Ways Fundraising, Fresh Pathways, NGO Fundraising and Rise Fundraising all entered liquidation or ceased trading after their PFRA memberships were terminated.[163]

Another worrying side issue is the exploitation of the fund raisers. An $85 million-$150 million class action was filed in late 2016 by Chamberlains Law Firm in conjunction with the National Union of Workers.[164] It is against leading fundraiser, Appco Group Australia, and at time of writing is proceeding through the Federal Court as a result of a decision by Mr. Justice Wigney on 18 May 2018.[165] Appco, which has raised funds for organisations such as the Starlight Foundation and Surf Life Saving Australia, unsuccessfully applied for a declaration that the claim was not properly commenced as a class action and that every case against it should be heard individually.

The company is accused of "sham contracting" – hiring charity workers to raise money for some of Australia's biggest charities as independent contractors rather than as employees to avoid paying minimum wages and entitlements. More than fourteen hundred participants in the forthcoming class action allege they were paid as little as $5 per hour for up to eighty hours per week.[166] The average claim value is reported to be $50,000.[167]

Appco is also accused of bullying charity collectors to collect more donations, providing sub-standard working conditions and subjecting collectors who failed to reach targets to humiliating rituals such as simulating sex acts and crawling around on the floor in what was called a "slug race".

Reports about Appco's behaviour have been circulating for years. It is reported that Appco has been investigated before for pocketing $7 million of the $12 million it collected for the Special Olympics Australia.[168] In 2015, it made a staggering $100 million in commission from charity collections.[169]

Here is one Channel 7 reporter's take on Appco:

> The third-party charity fundraising model in Australia is a sham ... something insupportable is happening across the country: the most munificent among us are being flagrantly and deliberately misled.

Donors are not being told that if they sign for a 12-month donation, up to 93% of that donation goes to Appco.[170]

These worrying developments around soliciting and getting donations bring into focus the issue of charity regulation.

The Shut-Eyed Sentry? The New Charity Regulator

From an international point of view Australia came quite late to the policy of national charity regulation. The Australian Charities and Not-for-profits Commission (ACNC) was not established until 3 December 2012.[171] Staples says that the ACNC was created with the support of the NGO sector to ensure accountability and transparency, to support good governance and innovation in the sector and to promote the reduction of unnecessary red tape:

> As far back as 1995, the sector was looking for these outcomes in submissions to an Industry Commission Report, *Charitable Organisation in Australia*. However, the idea was not pursued at the time, because NGOs feared the Howard government was not sympathetic to their democratic role as they saw it. It was not until 2007 under a Labor Government that they revived the idea of an independent body to regulate the sector. The UK Charities

Commission was seen as a model in the way it not only regulated NGOs, but also nurtured the sector with support programs to develop best practice. However, when the ACNC was set up in 2012, although described as an independent regulator, it became a statutory office under the umbrella of the ATO with a memorandum of understanding setting out the services the ATO undertakes for it.[172]

We shall see that the NGO's aspirations for increased accountability, transparency and good governance through a national charity regulator would remain fantasies.

Currently the *ACNC Act* limits registration to entities that are "charities" falling within the definition provided in the Act. The ACNC's name does not reflect its current functions. It does not have any regulatory reach into that vast and complex world of unregistered not-for-profit organisations that were considered in Chapter Two. However, it would be possible (indeed officially envisaged) to extend the regulatory framework in the future to cover NFPs without much trouble.[173] This will be an explosive development. If a resource starved ACNC cannot meet its regulatory obligations with respect to about 57,000 registered charities, how on earth is it going to be able to extend its reach to cover the 600,000 not-for-profit organisations in Australia?

Agency	**Staff Allocation**
Australian Securities and Investments Commission	1,656
Australian Financial Security Authority	487
Fair Work Commission	318
Aged Care Quality and Safety	316
Australian Skills Quality Authority	199
Australian Building and Construction Commission	155
Australian Human Rights Commission	122
Australian Charities and Not-for-profit Commission	**81**

Figure 8. Average staffing levels Commonwealth Regulators 2019.
The average number of employees receiving salary or wages (or compensation in lieu of these) over a financial year, with adjustments for casual and part-time employees to show the full-time equivalent. Source: Commonwealth Budget, 2019. https://www.budget.gov.au/2019-20/content/bp4/download/bp4_10_staffing.pdf

For a regulator, the ACNC has an unbalanced mix of responsibilities.[174] In 2017–18 only 11% of its staff budget of $15.85 million went to direct compliance services. This is roughly half the Commission's information technology budget for the same period![175] In 2017–18 the compliance division had a staff of 17.[176]

Figure 8 on the preceding page presents a random selection of staffing levels in some Commonwealth regulatory authorities. The purpose is not to make staffing comparisons, as each authority has a different purpose and a different constituency. However, the question remains: is the ACNC too small for its purpose?[177]

The ACNC is led by a Commissioner, two Assistant Commissioners, and a leadership team with access to an Advisory Board. In an unusual decision by government, and one that must have serious implications for the good governance of the regulator, Gary Johns, the current ACNC Chair, is allowed to operate on his own in an office in his hometown of Brisbane, while the rest of the ACNC staff are based in Melbourne. A very peculiar set of circumstances.

In the financial year up to June 2019, ACNC received 2,323 concerns about charities.[178] Like a stressed-out hospital emergency department, the ACNC must necessarily triage these complaints.

With the point about inadequate staffing levels already made, it is not surprising that 2,323 concerns about charity wrongdoing boiled down to just 12 registration revocations. Clearly the ACNC is not even scratching the surface of charity fraud.

What are the areas of concern that reach the regulator? The biggest field of complaints concerned charity workers obtaining a private benefit. This amounted to 37% of all complaints in the year to June 2019.[179] A hard to understand statistic (not included in the table opposite) is that charities with a religious purpose topped the list of those investigated (17%).[180]

The ACNC also has the power to revoke registration of charities that do not lodge two annual financial statements. Operating from a single office in Melbourne with only eighty one full time staff, of which there were only seventeen staff in the compliance section, one suspects that there is a lot of compliance work left undone.[181]

The revocation of charity status is amongst the strongest enforcement powers the ACNC has, and it is reserved for the most

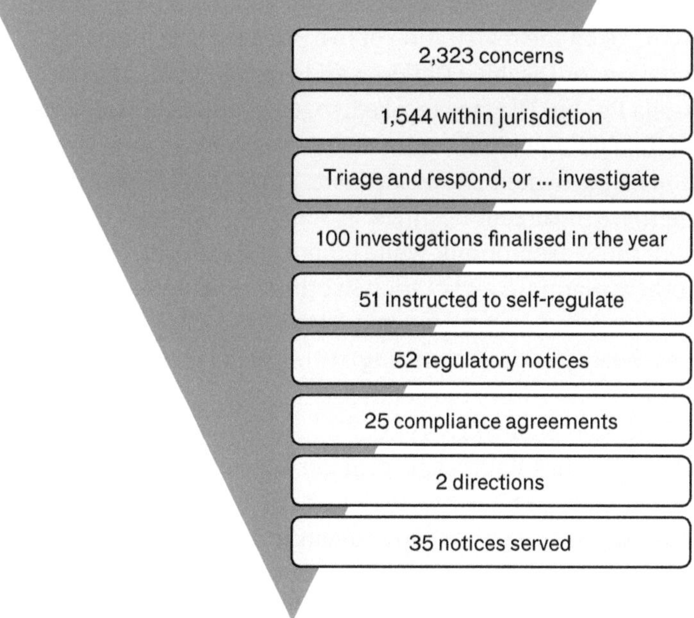

Source: G. Johns, "Addressing the Risk of Misuse in the Charity Sector." Presentation to the 7th Australian Public Sector Anti-Corruption Conference, Melbourne, 31 October 2019, Slide 6.

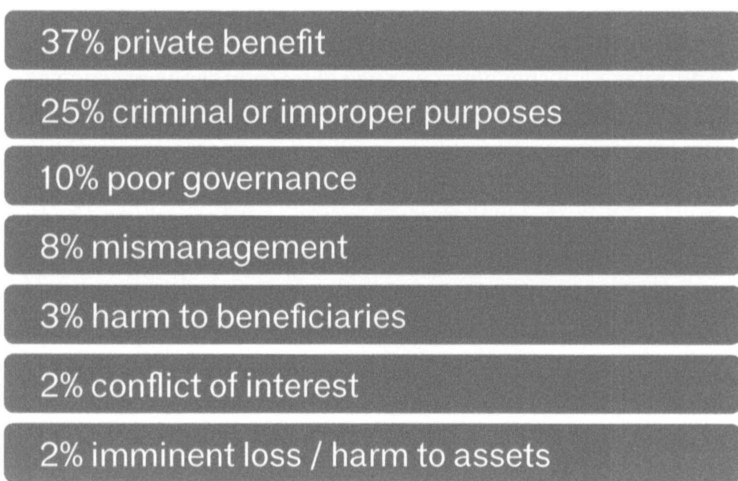

Source: G. Johns, "Addressing the Risk of Misuse in the Charity Sector." Presentation to the 7th Australian Public Sector Anti-Corruption Conference, Melbourne, 31 October 2019, Slide 7.

serious cases of misconduct or mismanagement. In May 2018, the ACNC revoked the registration of two charities; the Australian Foundation for Disabled Children and Youths Ltd and Pockets Australia Pty Ltd.[182] Once revoked, rogue charities are deprived of deductible gift recipient status, GST free purchases and income tax and fringe benefit tax exemptions. This is not necessarily the end of these miscreant charities, as some can continue to exist without these exemptions, while others rebrand and resurface, and others maintain registration in other jurisdictions. The abovementioned Australian Foundation for Disabled Children and Youths Ltd, at the time of writing, still appears to have a current operating licence from the South Australian Department of Consumer and Business Service.[183]

The ACNC has significant regulatory powers including the power to enter premises and to search, inspect, examine, retain or copy any document for gathering information to determine compliance or assess an applicant's entitlement to registration. It recently threatened the CEO of a large charity with imprisonment if he did not cooperate with ACNC investigators, although one suspects that there is a lot of bluff in this.[184] Failure to assist or attempts to circumvent the ACNC's information gathering and monitoring powers will amount to an offence also punishable by a $4,200 fine. The ACNC may conduct a compliance review or investigation which may result in advice, recommendations, or referrals to another agency or use of its formal powers such as giving directions (e.g. preventing the entering into transactions or the transferring of assets); accepting enforceable undertakings (including obtaining court orders); applying for injunctions to prevent contravention or to compel something to be done; suspending or removing responsible persons (or appointing an alternate person); issuing warnings and penalty notices; or revoking registration. Failure to comply with a requirement under the ACNC's enforcement powers is an offence punishable by financial penalty or imprisonment or both.[185]

These powers always seem impressive on paper. But in cold reality with, as mentioned, a staff of only eighty one (FTEs) and a budget allocation for 2017–18 down about $2 million from the previous year to $14.3 million, the ACNC must rely largely on self-assessment and denouncements.[186] When it does decide to investigate a charity, the aim is to have that investigation finished in six months. The very tight human resource situation at ACNC means this six months' time frame is officially only expected to be met 80% of the time. In the reporting period 2016–2017 the target was met only 64% of the time.[187] In the reporting period 2017–18 the situation had deteriorated with the target met only 50% of the time.[188] That's a troublingly low performance figure. It means that ACNC's compliance and investigation divisions were seriously undernourished during that reporting period. If for example the ACNC takes twelve months to close an investigation into a suspect charity, that is time enough for evidence to be destroyed and for the investigations to cease for want of proof. This all sounds like a good deal for charity fraudsters.

The Commonwealth Parliament did not give the ACNC powers of prosecution. Nor did it give the Commission powers to reclaim money that charities have obtained through fraud. Those powers reside in other jurisdictions. Again, these are significant deficits in the regulator's structure. Again, a boon to the charity crook.

What Parliament did give the Commission was a hard, inflexible culture of secrecy. The ACNC is not allowed to provide details of its enforcements.[189] It is quite remarkable that after decades of bi-partisan support for open government, the secrecy provisions in the ACNC Act preclude publication of the Commissioner's decisions even if those decisions have broader public interest or have precedent-guiding value.[190] The ACNC also allows charities to make applications for details of their operations to be withheld from the public. In 2017–18 the regulator accepted seven hundred and seventy one such applications.[191]

So, the donor community will never know what the Australian Foundation for Disabled Children and Youths Ltd and Pockets Australia Pty Ltd did to deserve licence revocation. Nor will it ever know the identity of the key players in these organisations, paving the way for these people to resurface in new criminal guises.[192]

The heavy canvas curtain of secrecy is also draped over charities referred to as "basic religious charities". These are the ones whose sole purpose is the advancement of religion. In 2016, there were nine thousand and twenty seven charities so registered with ACNC.[193] For a reason that appears to be lost in time, basic religious charities can keep their financial affairs secret. This immunity from disclosure obviously diminishes accountability. The recent review of the *Charities Act* and the ACNC recommended that this immunity be reviewed, not removed.[194]

While ACNC has national reach, it must interface with charities that operate under different State Acts. A clear example of this is the diversity in audit requirements between the States for charities that become incorporated associations. For example, in Queensland, incorporated charities that have annual revenue or assets in excess of $100,000 are required to be professionally audited, and those in the $20,000–$99,000 band must have their financial statements annually reviewed by an approved person.[195] In South Australia, the audit threshold is double that in Queensland[196] meaning that, theoretically, Queensland charities are twice as likely to be formally audited than their South Australian counterparts.[197]

Finally, we should heed Gary Johns' assessment of the ACNC's own regulatory environment. Because it speaks of a tightly bound regulator. In part of his presentation, "Welcome to my World", Johns outlined how his agency is a victim of bureaucratic capture (my words). Johns said that the ACNC is regulated by:

- 31 pieces of legislation
- 15 sets of regulations
- 79 policies and standards
- 53 ACNC policies and procedures
- ATO Chief Executive instructions
- 67 ISOs, plans and frameworks.[198]

So there you have it. A charity regulator, under-resourced and over-governed. Let's now take a look at the man himself. There are many ways to drive home the massive changes in the social provision landscape in Australia since its recapture by conservative forces. I choose to do so through focusing a biographical lens on Gary Johns, the new Chair the ACNC.

Gary Johns, ACNC Chair: Man of the Moment

The sub-title above may suggest that a glowing reference to Gary Johns is pending. I am not so much interested in his character as I am in his ideological development. Why? Because that development uncannily matches the ideological shift in public policy since the 1970s. Johns is the man in the river. We see him being swept along. He is moving fast, so is the river. He is not struggling. He seems to be enjoying the ride. The social and political landscapes were changing, so was Johns. He has gone from being a Labor politician to a senior fellow at the highly influential right wing think tank, the Institute of Public Affairs, to Chair of ACNC. These are the high points of Johns' career: he is a man in a river that is flowing to the Right.

As a young 35-year-old, Gary Johns won the north Brisbane working class seat of Petrie at the cliff-hanger 1987 Federal election. Only eight seats changed hands nationally at that election: Petrie was one of them. Johns represented Petrie until his defeat in 1996. Impressionable, ambitious, hard-working with a face that looks like it was chiselled from granite and a mouth like a folded arrest warrant, Johns was there almost at the start of the end of "old Labor".[199] At that time was he to know he was in a new paradigm?

His parliamentary apprenticeship would be served under the leadership of the populist but overrated Prime Minister, "good onya mate", Bob Hawke and his Treasurer sidekick with the smirk of a well-fed wolf, Paul Keating, the Labor man from Bankstown who dressed like a merchant banker and who once famously said that the best way to see Darwin is at 35,000 feet on the way to Paris. Together these two men changed the shape and purpose of government, *vis a vis* business, in ways so fundamental that nothing like it has come before or since.[200]

Johns' apprenticeship in this new market-loving paradigm lasted for six years until, in December 1993, he was appointed Assistant Minister for Industrial Relations. Notwithstanding that this was a junior appointment, Johns was on his way, and he never seemed to have minded that it was in a new paradigm. Labor men were discarding their work boots and kitting up real smart from Ermenegildo Zegna catalogues.

While the new Hawke–Keating paradigm can make some modest claims to welfare reform, the core of the paradigm was a dramatic stripping away of historical governmental services and obligations. Some of these developments have been considered in previous chapters. Outsourcing, privatisation and de-regulation were the new theme songs. Within a very short space of time government services either had "for sale" signs firmly planted on them, or were contracted out to business or, when they could not be flogged off or contracted out, made to become more efficient and bottom line sensitive, "just like business".

Under the new paradigm that Johns was starting to absorb, the Commonwealth Bank was sold off in 1996, after having been a government institution for 85 years.[201] QANTAS, CSL Limited, the Snowy Mountains Engineering Corporation, and more, were all sold off in the period of John's ideological apprenticeship. Australia Post was corporatized, and Optus was created to go head to head with Telecom (later Telstra), until Telstra too was sold off by the incoming Howard Government. An "accord" with the union movement, along with enterprise bargaining, allowed the Hawke–Keating paradigm to realise its full neo-liberal potential without union opposition.

By the end of the Hawke–Keating period the working-class parts of the electorate were fed up. In an extraordinary flip, John Howard brought the conservatives back to power in 1996 as the (false) champion of the Aussie battler. Big business, small government, this was the new order.[202]

Johns was defeated at the 1996 Federal election by the Liberal candidate, Teresa Gambaro. He soon secured employment with the most prominent right wing think tank in Australia, the Institute of Public Affairs.[203] As a senior fellow, he headed IPA's Non-Government Organisational Unit which was set up to investigate charities that attacked business. While many of his former Labor Party colleagues would have treated this move as treasonous, it was not so much an ideological transformation as the next step for the man in the river that was flowing to the Right.

> I always said you really belonged on our side Gary ... I'm sure we've got a spare blue T-shirt somewhere here we can give you ...

This statement sums up the public perception of Gary Johns. It was made in July 2015 by the (then) Liberal member for Petrie, Teresa Gambaro, as she launched Johns' book, *The Charity Ball. How to Dance to the Donors' Tune*, at a function organised by (another) right wing organisation, one that Johns is said to have started, the shadowy Brisbane-based Australian Institute for Progress.[204] Gambaro, it is recalled, defeated Johns in the 1996 election, but claims him now as a firm friend.

Johns' 2014 book sets out his views on charity. At the launch, Gambaro summarised it thus:

> In *The Charity Ball,* Gary quite rightly focuses on the need for donors to be better informed of the real purposes and goals of the many organisations and entities that are today calling themselves charities ...
>
> As Gary quite bluntly, but regrettably and very accurately puts it, too many charities in Australia do little or no charity work. Too many receive most of their income from government and too many lobby governments for even more.
>
> The 'charitable purpose' being pursued here is all too often the pursuit of the charity's own existence.
>
> What is even more ironic in this debate is that when the terrible spotlight of accountability and governance is applied to some charities, they cry foul and embark on a crusade of moral indignation railing against any who would dare question their legitimacy.[205]

Because of the compatibility between him and the then Turnbull Government on charities, especially on the need to keep a close watch on charity advocacy, the future Chair of the ACNC was starting to position himself ideologically for the job.

The determination to use all available means to shut noisy charities up was formed in the Howard years.[206] In 2003, on behalf of the IPA, Johns led a $50,000 government-funded consultancy inquiring into NGOs' relationships with the Federal Government called *The Protocol: Managing Relations with NGOs*. According to one commentator this report "was a blueprint for later repressive moves by the Howard Government against the sector".[207]

Three years after these comments in *The Charity Ball,* and three weeks after his appointment to the ACNC, Johns signed off on his Commission's submission to the mandated five years review of the government's new regulatory structure for charities.[208] In its submission the ACNC called for power to regulate the "effective use of the resources of not-for-profit entities". The Community Council for Australia's chief executive, David Crosbie, said the proposed objectives were "incredibly disappointing" and amounted to a "bizarre overreach" from the regulator. He said there was "no explanation" of how the ACNC would measure an "effective use of resources": "It's not the role of a government regulator which may not agree with a particular charity's approach – it's absurd that it should tell them how to use their resources", he said. "As long as charities are meeting their statutory requirements and fulfilling their charitable purpose it is not up to the regulator". He added: "The use of resources is best left up to charities, the communities they serve and their own governance structures".[209]

Crosbie then reflected on Johns' capacities, and he did not mince words:

> The ACNC commissioner is a very tough gig. It requires real expertise, personal capacity, and a commitment to enhancing the valuable work done in our charities sector. Dr Johns has demonstrated none of these characteristics. I fail to see how Dr Johns could manage an agency of over 100 dedicated staff, administer a complex set of laws and regulations, provide responsive services, reduce red tape and build community trust and confidence in the charities sector. Only a government committed to attacking the charities sector would put someone like Gary Johns in as head of the ACNC.[210]

What Crosbie did not say was that what was being revealed here was the second unofficial mission for ACNC. Along with the silencing of advocate charities, the government wants to be a player at the very centre of charity operations.

Johns certainly appears to have made a notable number of anti-charity statements in the time between separating from Labor in 1998 and being appointed as ACNC Chair. He is a straight talker, no stranger to controversy, and his remarks are appreciated. Not so much because he said them. But, rather, his comments are archetypal. He channels the new power perception of charities. We need to listen. In one of IPA's NGO watch publications, Johns expressed the view that charities interfere with the market and should be restricted.[211] In a 2002 article, he referred to "cashed up NGOs", describing them as "a dictatorship of the articulate" and a "tyranny of the minorities".[212] He also attacked their supporters, saying they were the "mail-order memberships of the wealthy left, content to buy their activism and get on with their consumer lifestyle".[213] In a 2001 IPA publication, he went so far as to question the need for NGOs in a democracy saying: "In democratic societies with accountable governments, strong regulation of the corporate sector and an absence of endemic corruption in business-government dealing, the role of NGOs is problematic".[214] It will be interesting to see how Johns reconciles his views with his statutory duties as ACNC Chair. Whichever way this observation is cut, there is no getting away from the mood within the charity community that they are tired of working within a flawed paradigm.

So, there he is. Gary Johns, moving from the left to the right at the same time the political tectonic plates were shifting back to a re-assertive and re-invigorated conservatism. He is, as I have said, a man in a river current, swept along, and making his own effort to get to a place very different from where he started. Now he is the boss of the charity regulator. What stamp will he place on that organisation?

The next two chapters profile four charities that have recently come to the attention of charity regulators, police and the courts for illegal activity. The cases have been specifically selected to illustrate the range of governance challenges across the wide spectrum of fraudulent operations.

Chapter Four
The Attack on Good Intentions: Three Case Studies

The trouble for capitalism is that the things that breed trust also breed the environment for fraud.

James Surowiecki.[215]

In this chapter, three charities are presented to illustrate the marked differences in charity fraud genres. The failed Shane Warne Foundation* is offered as an example of the *celebrity charity* model. This is followed by a case involving charity fraud at the highest levels of the New South Wales Returned and Services League (RSL). It is called *iconic charity* fraud because the corruption is incubated and protected in charities that come with a great amount of history and community respect. The third genre is called *key player fraud* because it involves the corrupt behaviour of individuals in positions of trust in otherwise law-abiding charities. The case illustrating this genre concerns the fraudulent actions of a person in a Gold Coast charity called Smart Employment Solutions and Living Options. Although we don't have the data, one gets the impression that *key player fraud* is the most common form of charity fraud.

The final chapter will offer deeper analyses of a charity that was destroyed by the corrupt actions of Eman Sharobeem, a charity fraudster of some note. Her undoing was the result of an exhaustive inquiry before the New South Wales Independent Commission against Corruption.

* It is important to state at the outset that no findings of charity fraud have been made against the Shane Warne Foundation. It is included because it perfectly illustrates the gross mismanagement risk embodied in the *celebrity charity* model.

Bowling for Benevolence: the Shane Warne Foundation

Shane Warne has chiselled himself into Australian popular history as one of the country's larrikins, both on and off the sporting field.[216] He played international cricket for Australia from 1991 to 2007. His bowling feats on the field earned him the title of the finest leg spinner in the world. With 708 wickets in 141 tests, he sits securely on a cricketing Mt. Olympus. Indeed, he has recently had a subterranean volcano in South Australia named after him in recognition of his explosive talent and fiery temperament![217]

Add those accomplishments to his doping fines, match suspensions, media silliness, high profile divorce and sexting to glamorous women, and we no longer have a man before us but a *celebrity*. In 2004, Shane Warne ("Warnie") got together with other "celebrities" and founded the Shane Warne Foundation with the high-minded intention of raising money to assist "seriously ill and underprivileged children and teenagers". The idea of the charity was quite simple, in fact, too simple. Entertain the well-heeled part of town with star-studded events such as celebrity poker games, make loads of money and give that money to selected charities such as the Starlight Foundation and Clown Doctors.

There is no evidence that the Foundation's celebrity board took expert advice. Perhaps what charity to endow and for how much was simply decided over long lunches. Compare this rudimentary allocation model to the charity run by Warne's old test skipper Steve Waugh. The Steve Waugh Foundation raises money for research into rare diseases. It allocates funds for that purpose guided by a high level medical advisory committee.[218]

After twelve years, the Shane Warne Foundation spluttered and crashed to earth in December 2016. This rise and fall story gives us some insights into "celebrity charities", a genre all on its own in the richly diverse world of good intention. Unlike charity scams set up by criminals with the clear intention of stealing money from donors, the motivation behind celebrity charities is more complex.

My efforts to access vital documents associated with the demise of the Shane Warne Foundation from Consumer Affairs Victoria under freedom of information virtually came to nought. Until an insider walks the story of the origins and workings of the

Shane Warne Foundation out into public glare we are left only with tantalising questions. What motivated Warne and his fellow luminaries on the Shane Warne Foundation Board (James Packer, Lloyd Williams, Ray Martin and Eddie McGuire, among others) to seek to improve the lot of vulnerable Australian children and teenagers? Did these millionaires fix their sights on vulnerable Australian children and teenagers on a whim or has the plight of these youngsters kept these men awake at night for a long period of time?

Along with this stellar presence on the Board, the Foundation also had "patrons" and "ambassadors" such as the Australian cricketer Michael Clark, the British actress and onetime fiancé of Warne, Elizabeth Hurley, the actor Russell Crowe and the perennial TV celebrity, Karl Stephanovic. Again, the same question: was a charitable purpose foremost in the minds of these celebrities when they agreed to become associated with the Foundation? We are entitled to this question because the Board was composed of people with real financial clout and people deeply embedded in very influential financial and political networks. We know from experience that powerful people with good intentions can be enormously beneficial to the community (think Andrew "Twiggy" Forrest).[219] So, what went wrong with the Shane Warne Foundation? Why weren't their impeccable contacts, indeed proportions of their considerable wealth, used to effect positive change amongst troubled youth? How come it folded so quickly? Maybe the real intention, the intention that stays shadowy, was for the Foundation to provide another platform for celebrity?

We don't know the answers to these questions *yet*. What we do know is the abysmal economic performance of the Foundation. The financial returns for 2014 show the Foundation spent $550,000 on fundraising amongst a cohort usually gracing the social pages of *New Idea*. But all this partying only raised $465,000.[220] The Foundation CEO, Shane Warne's brother Jason, was paid a salary of $80,000 in a year that saw only $54,600 distributed to beneficiaries.[221] With that sort of performance the regulator, Consumer Affairs Victoria (CAV), started to smell a rat.

According to reports, in October 2015, just weeks after the Foundation's footy final lunch where 600 people paid $200 a plate, the Foundation Board met in emergency session.[222] The Foundation had been running at a loss for four of the last five years and it could see the media and CAV coming for it with big questions.

In September 2015, the *Sunday Age* had applied for access to the Foundation's annual reports under an obscure section in the Victorian *Fundraising Act*. Partial access only was reluctantly given to the Foundation's economic reports which showed that between 2011 and 2013 the Foundation donated only sixteen cents in the dollar to beneficiaries.[223] The *Sunday Age* revealed that the Foundation had tried everything to avoid public scrutiny of its records, including making a failed application to the Federal Court to have its financial records sealed from public view under a provision to protect the privacy and security of family violence charities (which it was not).[224]

Meanwhile CAV wrote to the Foundation giving it until 29 February 2016 to submit audited reports for financial years July 2012 to July 2015 and 1 July to 31 December 2015.[225] On the same day as the deadline to produce audited reports, the Foundation released a media statement saying it was closing down. Undeterred, CAV wrote to the Foundation on 15 February 2016 advising them they must still do the audit. The next day the Foundation advised CAV that it had appointed KPMG and asked for extension of time. CAV granted an extension until 1 March 2016. On 11 March 2016, the Foundation sent the KPMG audit to CAV.

ABC News reported the next day that KPMG was "unable to draw conclusions on the foundation's cash donations due to its accounting practices".[226] KPMG found that while the Foundation had complied with most of its obligations, between 2012 and 2015 it did not meet requirements relating to lodgement and submission of its annual accounts. More worrying, KPMG found that because of limitations in gathering evidence and the nature of the charity's internal controls, "it was possible that fraud, error or non-compliance may occur but not be found".[227] In events not widely reported at the time, CAV, clearly not convinced by the KPMG audit, wrote to the Foundation on 10 May 2016 seeking more documents.[228] Still not getting what it wanted from the Foundation, CAV issued formal notices on 17 August 2016, this time seeking more records believed to include cash receipts.[229]

Running out of patience, CAV, in December 2016, sent a letter to the Foundation asking it to wind up.[230] Some two weeks later CAV, in clearing the Foundation of unlawful conduct, found that, "Over recent years ... a low proportion of funds raised have been distributed by the Foundation to beneficiaries. A cause of this was the high level of expenses when compared to income".[231]

The financial statement for 2016, the last reporting year of the Foundation before it folded, offers some interesting insights into how the charity was run. It reported total revenue of $628,727. Of this, fundraising income accounted for $470,334. This reflects the celebrity charity in action: big glitzy events for the big end of town. The fundraising expenses for the year ending 30 June 2016 amounted to $278,278. When that's added to a mysterious "professional fees" of $112,507, and an equally mysterious "other expenses" of $81,334 we find that it took the Foundation $472,119 to earn the year's income of $628,727.[232] So for every dollar raised only twenty five cents got to the nominated charities. The question, "Who is benefiting?" becomes irresistible now.

The directors of the Foundation at the time were Shane Warne (chair), Ann Peacock (Melbourne socialite and the public relations face of the ethically challenged Crown Casino),[233] David Evans (founder and executive chair of investment advisory company Evans and Partners, non-executive director of Seven West Media), Andrew Basset (co-founder of Seek.com), Glen Robbins (well-known Australian comedian) and Eddie Maguire (Australian radio and television personality and president of Collingwood Football Club). This is a blue-chip list of movers and shakers, some of whom run multi-million-dollar corporations. Yet they couldn't run a small charity?

For all its talk about transparency, Consumer Affairs Victoria has kept the greater proportion of its regulatory dealings with the Shane Warne Foundation secret. It certainly failed the accountability test when it made no mention of the actions it took against the Shane Warne Foundation in its 2016–17 Annual Report.

We don't know, but should know, core facts: did the Foundation have staff? Who were they? What were their qualifications to run a charity? We know that Shane Warne's brother had a paid position with the Foundation in 2014. Is it possible that it is his name that has been redacted from the 2014 financial statement?[234]

We also know that in 2015 for a short period, Stacie Childs, a former employee of the Melbourne Storm Football Club, was the Foundation's nominated "key personnel". But that's all we know. How did the Foundation choose charities to fund? Did the Foundation run full-time or part-time? Its last recorded office address was Level 3, 199 Toorak Road Melbourne. This is the location of Sy Group Chartered Accountants. The Foundation said that the space it rented there was owned by one of the Foundation's directors. The yearly rent for 2016 was $24,207.[235] The Foundation said that this rent was decided on an arm's-length basis. This could be a lie, or it could show the Foundation infrastructure so shallow as to be meaningless. 199 Toorak Road Melbourne is one of Australia's premier locations. It was sold in November 2010 for $20 million. In August 2018 a 145 square metre space at that address was offered for rental for $95,000 per year.[236] With those numbers in the background, the Foundation's rental costs are substantially out of market. The only other possibility is that the Foundation only used a desk, chair and phone in the offices of Sy group Chartered Accountants. We know when it was wound up the Foundation only had plant and equipment to the value of $8,887. How can you run a *real* charity with such limited resources?

Celebrity charities use their glitz power to talk up real action against want. Celebrities can open hearts and wallets better and faster than most. The celebrity charity model is, however, deeply flawed because "celebrity" and "charity" are irreconcilable concepts. "Celebrity" conjures a world of hype, big money and glamour people in glamour locations. "Celebrity" also implies no special understanding of the complex requirements in being part of an organisation that has charitable purposes. The celebrity charity model also requires these same people to embrace "charity", another world, where commitment to righting a wrong, or filling a gap in services or correcting an injustice, are central to the job description. It takes a special kind of celebrity to bridge between "celebrity" and "charity". Some do. But when celebrity charities fail, they do so because the people concerned cannot manage the irreconcilabilities. In this respect the Shane Warne Foundation follows into disrepute other high profile celebrity charities like rock star Bono's African anti-poverty charity, ONE, and Lady Gaga's Born this Way Foundation. The flaws in the celebrity charity model are not shared with the next case, which incorporates its own set of flaws.

Soldiers of Misspent Fortune: Corruption in the New South Wales RSL

> It has been particularly difficult for the members ... to accept that [Mr. Don Rowe] the former President of RSL NSW, an organisation charged with looking after needy and/or homeless veterans, would use its money to fund his personal lifestyle and that of his family. It has been a great shame for the organisation.
>
> It is all very well to admit, as Mr Rowe did, that the use of RSL NSW funds in this manner was "wrong". However, his attempt to maintain that such conduct was not "deliberate" was an unimpressive episode in his evidence which exposed his failure to come to grips with the gravamen (*Bergin Inquiry*).[237]

Contagion-like, Returned and Services League (RSL) branches in various parts of Australia have recently come to the attention of state charity watchdogs, government inquiries and the national charity regulator, the ACNC, for fraud and serious governance failings. In August 2017, the ACNC completed an investigation into RSL South Australia, after the organisation put itself into voluntary administration following a mounting cash crisis, resignations and Board upheavals.[238] The ACNC investigation resulted in the charity entering into a compliance agreement with the regulator. The ACNC issued another direction to RSL Queensland on 29 March 2018 after an investigation into the charity also found serious governance failures and that the charity was dragging its feet in meeting the required Governance Standards set by ACNC.[239] ACNC Commissioner, Gary Johns, said that the ACNC's own investigations, and the Bergin Inquiry (see below), had detailed serious governance and accountability issues: "Unfortunately, poor governance practices and misconduct have been far too common in the past, and this has damaged the reputation of one of Australia's most well-known charities", Johns said. On 19 July 2018, the President of RSL National, Mr. Robert Dick, resigned after the ACNC announced in February 2018 that it was starting an investigation into RSL National.[240]

While the previous case illustrated issues uniquely associated with celebrity-based charities, the RSL case illustrates what happens when a charity is, and has been for many years, riding (and exploiting) a crest of public trust and approval. RSL National was established way back in 1916 because of the need to support those diggers returning from the bloody carnage of Gallipoli and the Western Front in World War I, and the families of those who did not return. RSL LifeCare is even older, having been established in 1911.[241]

RSLs share this historical space with other hallowed charities which have been around for a long time such as the St. Vincent de Paul Society, Anglicare and the Australian Red Cross. Times are changing. Where once the community extended an enormous latitude to these charities, now their high approval may no longer be a firewall against public disapproval and reputational damage. The threshold is coming down. A clear exemplar of this point is obviously the forensic confidence with which the Royal Commission into Institutional Responses to Sexual Abuse exposed many of these historical charities.[242] Such an inquiry would not have been possible twenty years ago.

The Bergin Inquiry

Following a number of embarrassing stories in the *Sydney Morning Herald* and on the ABC, and just 24 hours after receiving a second report from forensic auditors, KordaMentha, nine directors of the scandal-plagued RSL NSW were internally charged by the RSL National Board on 17 January 2017 with bringing the organisation into disrepute.[243] This unenthusiastic initiative at the RSL national level was soon superseded with urgent government intervention. The New South Wales Government found it could not hold back a surge of media interest and questions from concerned people. It had to act. On 15 May 2017, it appointed the Hon. PA Bergin SC to inquire into the New South Wales Branch of the Returned and Services League of Australia.[244]

RSL NSW is a massive operation. It has approximately 40,000 members throughout New South Wales, belonging to any of 352 RSL NSW sub-branches. Each sub-branch has a certain fundraising autonomy which makes a nightmare of the question, "Where is all the money coming from and where is it going?"

RSL NSW oversees several subsidiaries including: 135 Women's Auxiliaries, 65 RSL Day Clubs and 39 RSL Youth Clubs. A fact not widely known is that RSL NSW is also a mega business managing interests in approximately 150 properties, including, and most contentious of all, the Hyde Park Inn, a 97 room, four-star hotel which it owns outright, right in the heart of Sydney. RSL NSW has responsibility for managing financial assets of approximately $400 million.[245]

This begs some simple questions, which can also be applied to other mega charities: is the RSL a big business or a big charity? How can a not-for-profit organisation justify this extraordinary level of asset accumulation? Is it impossible to manage the contradictory requirements of an organisation being both a business and a charity? I return to this matter shortly.

At the beginning of her six hundred and ninety-eight-page report into RSL NSW the Hon. PA Bergin offered a chilling update on what she had exposed:

> Each [RSL] entity has made admissions of non-compliance with the Act, the relevant Charitable Fundraising Regulations and their respective fundraising authorities. Each entity has suspended all charitable fundraising within its organisation from August 2017 until further notice. [246]

To suspend fundraising is like ordering a person to stop breathing. If the culpable state directors of RSL NSW thought that this ploy was going to save them they were in for a big surprise. After examining all the evidence Bergin was scathing:

> There have also been investigations into the State Presidential Expenses Policy of RSL NSW; the expenses incurred by the former President of RSL NSW, Mr Donald Rowe; the use by Mr Rowe of an RSL NSW credit card; and the circumstances surrounding Mr Rowe's resignation and its aftermath ... Mr Rowe gave evidence admitting misuse of the RSL NSW credit card and improper conduct in dealing with expenses that were funded or reimbursed by RSL NSW.

Bergin also spoke directly about the cover-up, which is always a feature of troubled charities facing reputational damage:

> Between 2014 and 2017, RSL NSW pretended to its members and the public that the only reason Mr Rowe resigned was ill health, when the truth was that but for being confronted with questions about his expenses he would not have resigned at that time. The misleading statements that were published that his resignation was for reasons of ill health were embellished with statements from various RSL NSW State Councillors and officers and the RSL National President of warm wishes of gratitude for Mr Rowe's wonderful service and for a speedy return to good health. The State Councillors, with the encouragement of the RSL National President, acted in part to protect the good name of the RSL or the 'RSL Brand'. They were also motivated to protect themselves from criticism. Their actions have had the opposite effect. The cover up has besmirched the good name of the RSL and damaged the individual reputations of the State Councillors involved.[247]

The evidence that the Bergin Inquiry found: the cover-up of Mr Rowe's conduct; the false and misleading statements issued by and on behalf of RSL NSW about Mr Rowe's resignation; the faulty mechanisms of approving the presidential expenses; the inability to trace publicly donated funds through its financial records; and the abysmal failures to comply with the legislation and the fundraising authorities amounted to grounds:

> ... upon which the Minister could be satisfied ... that RSL NSW was not a fit and proper entity to administer or be associated with a fundraising appeal for charitable purposes.[248]

The Inquiry also found massive conflicts of interest, with the directors of RSL LifeCare approving their own consultancy contracts and approving the increases in their own consulting fees over many years. This, the Inquiry observed:

> ... also provides grounds upon which the Minister could be satisfied that RSL LifeCare was not a fit and proper entity to administer or be associated with a fundraising appeal for charitable purposes.[249]

These scathing conclusions brought RSL NSW to the precipice. Why didn't it fall into the abyss? If these recommendations from the Bergin Inquiry had been enacted, that surely would have been the result. That RSL NSW survived is explained in two ways. First, to repeat the mantra from the 2007 global financial crisis, RSL NSW was "too big to fail". Secondly, and related to the first, there was no political will to wind up the entity. Not only would there have been a severe kickback from the voters, but the government would have been faced with the impossible task of taking over the RSL's welfare burden. If this gloomy analysis is correct it means that our hallowed charities can withstand the severest storms. This surely distinguishes the hallowed charities from their smaller counterparts with no history. With the smaller charities, the community, jaded by scams, often implements a "one strike and you are out" policy.

What specifically happened in RSL NSW? Forensic auditing specialists, KordaMentha (KMF), were brought in to plumb the depths of the corruption. They discovered, as is often the case, gross credit card abuse. Expenses on former RSL NSW president Rowe's RSL credit card were $465,376.[250] This included cash withdrawals of $214,050.[251] These withdrawals were described as "business expenses" with no supportive documentation. In one 6-year period Rowe incurred approximately $40,000 in telephone bills, many of which were for personal calls made by him and his family.[252] He purchased meals for RSL State Councillors and his family, contrary to the spending guidelines.[253] He allowed his family to stay often in the State President's suite in the RSL-owned Hyde Park Inn.[254] He even allowed his son to live in that suite rent free for seven years![255]

Rowe's private spending on his corporate credit card came to the attention of his archrival, Mr. Rod White, then RSL State Treasurer.[256] White was not coming to this confrontation with clean hands. He was one of the directors found to have taken money from the RSL under the guise of "consultancy fees", an issue considered below.[257] White was told by the internal auditor about Rowe using the RSL credit card to pay for family Optus bills. In the scheme of the wrongdoing these were paltry amounts. As giants can trip on small things, so did Rowe. This expenditure led to Rowe's downfall as the following extract so vividly paints:

> I [White] said Don [Rowe] what's this about? ... I said look, I've got an envelope here Don and in this envelope is some matters relating to your expenses do you want me to open it? And that's

> when ... Don said, please don't open it, and I said well you know what's in here, and I said this is about phones and a few other things and I said Don, I think we've got to start going back through your expenses and he looked at me with tears in his eyes and said please don't. At that point, I said well Don, I've had enough, ... either you go today or I go today and if I go today, I've got to go and let State Council know, I'll go and see Chris, and I'll go and see Annette, but by Jeez I ain't [*sic*] going to let this go under the carpet. At that point he said I'll leave today.[258]

KMF also found that between 2007 and 2016, RSL LifeCare made payments totalling $2,552,751 (camouflaged as "consulting fees") to eight of the RSL NSW State Council members who were simultaneously directors of RSL LifeCare.[259] Interestingly, KMF also found an ascending frequency of wrongdoing. In other words, the number of directors of RSL LifeCare who were paid consulting fees over the years did not level out or decrease. KMF found it got worse over time: from 31% of directors receiving these illicit "consultancy fees" in 2006 to 100% of directors doing so in 2015.[260] This suggests that this gross stealing of donated funds was normalised over time in the RSL NSW State Council.

Normalisation of corruption is an interesting but little understood phenomenon.[261] Specifically applied here to RSL NSW, the normalisation of corruption is a cultural process that sanitises criminal behaviour. Ashforth and Vikas explain that three processes are operating to get to the stage where *all* directors were stealing money from RSL NSW. The first process is *institutionalisation*, where an initial corrupt decision or act becomes embedded in structures and processes and thereby routinised. This is usually driven from the top. In other words, the most powerful player starts the corrupt routine. This gives underlings moral "permission" to engage unethically. *Institutionalisation* is overlayed by a second process Ashforth and Vikas call *rationalisation*, where self-serving viewpoints held by the Directors act to justify and perhaps even valorise corruption. The third overlayed process is called *socialisation*, where naive newcomers are introduced early to a view that accessing RSL funds is as morally neutral as withdrawing one's own money from an ATM machine.

The Bergin Inquiry gives us excellent forensic detail of the rationalisation process in action. Rowe's escapades with his RSL credit card threatened to blow into a firestorm. The RSL's gut reaction was damage control. To that end an extraordinary RSL NSW State Council meeting was held on 27 January 2015. The National RSL President, Kenneth Doolan (a retired Rear Admiral) addressed the meeting after instructing that all microphones be turned off:[262]

> Around Australia in the RSL, myself included, are lots of people trying hard as volunteers, you all are trying hard as volunteers and one of the things every now and again is that people make mistakes. My aim as your National President whilst I'm in that job is to try to get people to say well OK, move on, accept that people make mistakes. If it's criminality, it's criminality, and then I've had sub branch, branch presidents ring me up by saying it should go to the DPP, a criminal matter, simple as that. But if it's an honest error of judgement something that people shouldn't have done, I ask people to look at it in the context of what people have done over the years, around this table sitting here, God knows how many years of volunteer service by all of you not only around this table but in your Sub-Branches and other places as well. I think we owe it to ourselves and the good name of the RSL to think in those terms. ... That [Rowe matter] was corrected in time because the State authority came in and took over. We are self-corrected. But be generous please in looking at those who put a lot of work into something over the years.[263]

Doolan left the special RSL NSW State Council meeting after making this statement.

Before returning to that meeting, a side observation is made to illustrate how charities can take a long time to de-corrupt themselves. Four months after Patricia Bergin began her forensic excavation, Doolan himself was in hot water. The news broke about Doolan at the worst possible time for the NSW RSL. It was when each day's evidence of NSW RSL fraud from the Bergin Inquiry was on the news that night. Some three years after making his let bygones be bygones speech to the NSW RSL State Council, it was reported that the RSL National Board was investigating whether Doolan, on his retirement as RSL National President in June 2016, had accepted a car valued at almost $27,500 and books to the value of $3,000 out of RSL funds.[264] Robert Dick, Doolan's successor as National President, stood aside during the investigation. Dick's claim that the gifts were entirely proper again depended on the rationalisation argument:

> [The gifts were] within the guidelines of the RSL constitution ... Now the national president does not receive an honorarium and Mr. Doolan had been there for seven to eight years.[265]

Again, what was to be a quiet little internal inquiry about these gifts was superseded by an ACNC investigation which found that the gift-giving was improper and ordered NSW RSL to address its non-compliance. A month after the *Bergin Report* was tabled in the New South Wales Legislative Assembly, ACNC, the charity regulator, ordered NSW RSL to appoint a governance expert and present to it an action plan within four months of appointing the expert. Clearly ACNC was concerned.[266] Doolan himself gave evidence at the Bergin Inquiry about the retirement gifts and said that he "... felt particularly uncomfortable and would have preferred my colleagues would have not done so".[267]

After Doolan left that special RSL NSW State meeting in January 2015, the Council went into committee to discuss the forensic audit on Rowe's spending that had been provided to them. It is clear that the councillors were conflicted. Some were persuaded by Doolan's arguments, others were not. One councillor, Mr James, noted that the review not only showed that a serious indictable offence had been committed but RSL NSW was exposed to the offence of concealing a serious indictable offence. He suggested that one option that was available to the State Council was to forward the review findings to the NSW Police.[268]

The Council referred the matter to its legal counsel, John Cannings of Price Waterhouse Cooper. His view was that, notwithstanding the fact that Rowe had unauthorised expenses on his RSL credit card, "he did not do so with the requisite intent to amount to 'fraudulent' or 'criminal' behaviour ... the breaches were at worst careless".[269]

Cannings' advice was heeded and the RSL State Council went into shut down. RSL members and media were lied to as State Council spread the story that Don Rowe had resigned for medical reasons. The Bergin Inquiry went on to recommend that the Minister refer the thirteen State Councillors to ASIC and the ACNC for their involvement in covering up Mr Rowe's misuse of RSL NSW funds.[270] The Inquiry also recommended that the Minister refer Don Rowe to the NSW Police.

The Bergin Inquiry exposed the financial wrongdoing of the RSL NSW State President, Don Rowe and the cover-up by his colleagues on State Council. However, Bergin's work was not complete. There was still the matter of State Councillors paying themselves lucrative "consultancy" fees.[271] This part of the saga is particularly interesting for two reasons. First, we see a payola culture emerge very quickly within State Council with next to no ethical anguishing about the morality of stealing donated funds for private purposes. Secondly, we see much energy was expended on how to make stealing donated funds look legal, so no-one ended up on the front pages of the *Sydney Morning Herald*, or in jail. The State Councillors did not do this on their own. They received rolling legal and financial advice from high fee charging experts who must have known what the real intent of the State Councillors was.

The precedent that led to the "consultancy" fee saga began in 1997 when RSL LifeCare accepted an outside report and appointed two paid consultants to the Board. It was explained at the time that RSL LifeCare needed the benefit of advice from experts in the field of aged accommodation. Prior to that the Board of RSL LifeCare consisted of the RSL NSW State President as an ex officio member and other persons appointed by RSL NSW. At that time, the directors were generally appointed from the ranks of State Councillors.

In early 2001, RSL LifeCare was seeking legal advice from Mr. Cannings on the topic of "directors' remuneration". Cannings said that while the RSL Constitution forbade directors being paid for their "ordinary services", he believed a case could be made for payment to directors for "extraordinary services".[272] This was the birth of a policy that would heap an enormous amount of opprobrium on RSL NSW. The policy was clearing the way for State Council directors to have the best of both worlds: a personal money stream from the RSL cash cow that was falsely characterised as constitutional.

Up until 2006 this policy was restricted to bringing outsiders onto the LifeCare Board and remunerating them $12,500 for their specialist contributions. In July 2006, RSL LifeCare received a letter from Mercer Human Resource Consulting Pty Ltd that provided advice in relation to "fee levels for directors". Mercer advised that, in their experience, many not-for-profit organisations did not pay any remuneration to board members as they were happy to donate their time and gain the experience of contributing to the board. Mercer also advised that it was only where organisations were more "commercial" and/or the board were active in advising on the assets of the organisation that fees were paid to the board members. This advice suited the RSL powerbrokers of an organisation morphing from a charity into a mega business.

The Board meeting for 22 August 2006 discussed the Mercer Report and decided on a change of tactics for the directors to receive remuneration. They appeared to have abandoned for the time being the fiction between "ordinary" (unpaid) and "extraordinary" (paid) tasks and resolved to seek advice from John Cannings, their trusted legal advisor, over ways to change the RSL Constitution to allow remuneration to Board directors.[273] Cannings advised that a constitutional change had to be passed by special resolution of the members of RSL LifeCare in a general meeting. He further advised that any member who is remunerated or receives a benefit was not entitled to vote in respect of such resolution or be present at the meeting, when the details of the remuneration would be considered; and a quorum could not be properly constituted if the number of members of the governing body who were proposed to be remunerated exceeded one third. This was a dangerous course. It risked inflaming those members who saw RSL LifeCare as a benevolent organisation led by people who donated their time free for the good of the charity. What was needed to get the directors access to the RSL cash cow was a strategy that had a surface plausibility and was above all secret.

Thus was born the third iteration of the game called, "How do us Directors get paid without RSL people, charity regulators and the media asking awkward questions?" Cannings was advised that the Board "... would now like to review the potential to pay specialist consulting fees to consultants, some of whom are directors. As you are aware, this is currently in place for 'non-RSL' directors. The Board would like to extend this potential to all directors".[274] Cannings replied in late November 2006 that he saw no constitutional impediment to the new proposal as long as certain inflammable issues such as full disclosure of pecuniary benefit and conflict of interest were controlled.

Cannings also advised that the mechanism by which the consultancy services could be provided was through advisory committees on which the directors who possessed the "relevant specialist skills" could serve. Then he said that such advisory committees could be established by resolution of the directors identifying the particular purpose of the advisory committee and specifying the general tasks to be carried out by those committees.[275] Here is the climax. From the directors' pay scandal moving like a slow waltz from 1997 to 2006, Cannings' suggestion this time heated the corruption up to tango proportions. What in effect could happen now is that the directors could not only quietly appoint themselves as consultants, and (audaciously) nominate their own remuneration. They could also design their own committees tailored to whatever talents they thought they had rather than the needs of RSL LifeCare.

Was the avarice to stop there? Apparently not. All of the directors who were keen to access the new income stream had their payments *backdated*. On 19 June 2007 Mr Rod White, the RSL State Treasurer, received a payment of $18,000, which was the annual fee under his new consultancy agreement, for the year ending 30 June 2007. This meant that he was in fact paid consulting fees backdated to 1 July 2006, which was before the Board of RSL LifeCare had even considered the issue of consulting fees being extended to the State Councillor directors, including Mr White.[276]

The new consultancy arrangements were anchored with individual contracts. Each director had to nominate the areas of "specialist advice" that they were offering to RSL LifeCare. Rod White's contract illustrated the sham nature of this consultancy arrangement. His areas of specialist advice included "ex-service, welfare and benevolence and general management experience".[277] We can see the fraud clearly now. Where once these areas of expertise were regarded as part and parcel of the ordinary competencies a director of the RSL was assumed to have, now these areas are reclassified as specialist, and monetarised.

Not content with this sham scheme now operating for the sole benefit of the directors, submissions were made to allow these payments to come through the RSL's salary packaging arrangements, allowing the directors to minimise the tax paid on their "consultancy fees". The line appears to have been drawn on this ploy. However, in early 2010 the directors gave themselves the usual annual income boost, with Mr. White now receiving around $30,000 for "consultancy fees"; and also awarded themselves an additional $5000 over three years for "tools of trade".[278] These pay arrangements continued to June 2017. Then, what the directors feared most, regulatory and media attention on their consultancy arrangements, started to occur.

The person expressing most anxiety about this was the CEO of RSL LifeCare, Ron Thompson. The unravelling started in June 2015 when Thompson asked Price Waterhouse Coopers (PwC) to externally review the fees paid to directors. It was apparent at this time that none of the directors were furnishing to RSL LifeCare information about actual hours spent that would justify their consultancy fees.[279] In March 2016, Mr Thompson wrote to PwC: "The directors themselves have a significant conflict of interest. I also have a (smaller) conflict of interest".[280]

The media and the charity regulator, the ACNC, finally became attentive to the directors' fees issue as well. As a result, payment of "consultancy fees" was suspended and all the consultancy agreements terminated in October 2016. But this was not the action of an organisation trying to correct its veer into wrongdoing. It was the action of an organisation determined to continue a wrong practice but laying low until the cops were off the beat. The Board resolution of 7 June 2017 resolved that a letter be issued by the company to any director retiring from the Board and having had a payment suspended under a Consultancy Agreement confirming that: a) the Company considers such Consultancy Agreement to be validly entered into and legally binding; b) payments suspended in respect of services rendered will be accrued by the Company in its accounts; and c) the Company intends to pay amounts accrued following the conclusion of the ACNC and Bergin inquiries subject to there being no legal impediment to doing so.[281]

There is other strong evidence that the cover up of the "consultancy" fees extended to the RSL's own members. When one of the executive team, Mr. Toussaint, raised the issue of directors being paid in early 2015, he was threatened by Mr. White, the RSL NSW State President, who was one of the principal beneficiaries of the illicit scheme. White demanded that Toussaint withdraw the allegation and then sent an email to Mr Toussaint on 21 May 2015 (copied to the other State Councillors), demanding that he refrain from repeating the allegations unless he could provide supporting evidence; and threatening him with "every possible action".[282]

Thirteen RSL NSW State Directors who were paid "consultancy" fees were examined before the Bergin Inquiry.[283] Each was asked the same set of questions as to when they became sensitised to the issue that participating in the decision-making as to what level of remuneration they should receive constituted a conflict of interest. Dr. Macri's answers here are typical of how other directors answered this set of questions.

Dr Macri was asked about the Minutes of the RSL LifeCare Board meeting on 20 February 2007 in which it was noted that the current persons receiving specialist consulting fees would receive new and revised contracts. She gave the following evidence:

> **Q.** You would accept then that you were voting in relation to a matter that concerned your own consulting fees; correct?
> **A.** Correct.
> **Q.** Knowing what you know today, you would recognise that as being a conflict of interest, that position that you were in; correct?
> **A.** Correct.
> **Q.** Would I be right to say that that was something that did not occur to you at the time?
> **A.** That's right.
> **Q.** Do you now accept that it ought to have done?
> **A.** Absolutely.
> **Q.** When was the first time that you became aware that there was any possibility of there being a conflict of interest in directors voting in respect of contracts concerning their own consulting fees?
> **A.** When the Inquiry started.
> **Q.** So in May of this year?
> **A.** That's right.[284]

The standout issue here, and one that really puzzles, is the persistent and apparently unanimous moral blindness of the directors until they were caught in the harsh glare of the Bergin Inquiry. Unfortunately, the questioning at the Bergin Inquiry did not go deeper into the cultural setting within the RSL NSW LifeCare Board that spawned and perpetuated this moral blindness.

John Cannings has figured prominently in this narrative to date. He was the legal advisor to RSL NSW and RSL LifeCare from 2001. Some of his evidence at the Bergin Inquiry was exposed as "very unsatisfactory".[285] Until he gave evidence at the Inquiry it was understood that Cannings was the honorary legal advisor to both entities. At the Inquiry, Cannings' claim that he had no recollection of ever being an honorary legal advisor conflicted with his application for one of the vacant directorships at RSL LifeCare:

> I have been a corporate and commercial lawyer for the past 32 years and involved with the Returned and Services League of Australia (New South Wales Branch) for the past 29 years (18 as Senior Honorary Legal Adviser) and as Honorary Legal Adviser to LifeCare for the past 14 years. I intend to retire from PwC from 30 June 2016 and as such I am permitted to take on Board roles in my last year. If I were to be appointed to the Board prior to 30 June 2016 I would cease my role as Honorary Legal Adviser from that date.[286]

The fact is that PwC and Mr. Cannings charged fees to RSL NSW and RSL LifeCare that amounted to approximately $8 million in the period 2007–2016.[287]

In early 2016 Cannings, through his company ICAN Consulting Pty. Ltd, contracted with RSL LifeCare to provide various services at board and committee level. In November 2016 Cannings retired from PwC. In January 2017 Cannings submitted a tax invoice and timesheet for the period March–December 2016 for $27,279. For 38.25 hours work, this equated to $731 per hour.[288] When Cannings was appointed to the RSL LifeCare Board in March 2017 he requested that this invoice be torn up. Shortly after this he raised another invoice, this time for $39,000 for services rendered in the period August 2016–January 2017. He was adamant that this was for non-legal services to RSL LifeCare. If he had provided either legal or consulting services between August and 30 November 2016 a proportion of the fee should have gone to his firm PwC, as he remained a partner until 30 November 2016.[289] The Inquiry found Cannings evidence around this topic "unimpressive".

The final recommendation from the part of the Bergin Inquiry that related to the illicit "consultancy" fees issue was that, of the thirteen RSL LifeCare Board members who took these payments, seven should be referred to the Minister for Innovation and Better Regulation, the Honourable Matthew Kean MP, for action by the business regulator, the Australian Securities and Investments Commission and the charity regulator, ACNC. Thompson, the CEO, was also referred. Inexplicably, Cannings was not.[290]

Bergin submitted her scathing report in January 2018, after thirty six hearing days and thirty five witnesses. We sit back now, in an attitude of scepticism, as the report tracks through to police and regulators. It will be a while before we know whether Bergin stimulated a real de-corruption of NSW RSL. Or will the crooks caught in the spotlight slip the noose and scurry down the steps of the gallows?

One possible answer is found in the way a reforming manager was treated when he attempted to change the culture of entitlement in NSW RSL. In August 2015, Glenn Kolomeitz, a lawyer and former soldier with postings in Afghanistan and East Timor, was appointed the new CEO of NSW RSL. The organisation was under siege. Its corrupt president, Don Rowe, had been forced out in November 2014, scandal was in the air and new allegations of donation stealing were flowing like sewerage. Kolomeitz thought he had a wide sanction to get NSW RSL back on moral track. He was dead wrong.

He ordered a full forensic audit in September 2016, saying at the time, "I didn't realise the depth of the governance problems I'd have to start fixing".[291] In interviews, Kolomeitz makes repeated references to a culture of entitlement in the NSW RSL: "The sending of the executives and their wives to Thailand (to visit the factory that was making their blazers) was disgraceful", he said. He was also appalled at another little scheme he came across whereby RSL members were issued with $500 beer cards when they renewed their membership.[292] He recalls an ex-digger saying to him, "I fought at Long Tan and you took my beer card away". He was also appalled at the gathering wealth of some of the sub-branches:

> Maroubra sub-branch are sitting on $28 million from the sale of an asset on my watch; that's $1million per young veteran who has taken his life this year alone.[293]

Finally, Kolomeitz reported NSW RSL to the NSW police for forging his signature in a ballot. The entire NSW RSL Council stepped down in February 2017. In a move that makes a mockery of New South Wales whistleblower protection laws, Kolomeitz was sacked by a caretaker Board on 3 May 2017 ostensibly for a contractual breach.[294] The date is significant: the sacking was just two weeks before the Bergin Inquiry was due to start. The New South Wales Opposition leader, Luke Foley, tweeted, "@RSLNSW sack CEO Glenn Kolomeitz. – Vindictive and inappropriate given current enquiry into organisation. Veterans deserve better".

Two months later, NSW RSL publicly apologised for his sacking and gave him $300,000 compensation and the ownership of the Mercedes car that he, as CEO, was officially allocated. This last point, an RSL senior manager driving around in a Mercedes, is indicative of how far the RSL has morphed from charity to big business. Kolomeitz's own language, liberally sprinkled with words like "brands", "corporate focus", "good business modelling", "marketing", "corporate partnerships" testifies to this.

The RSL case centred on a conspiracy of individuals in a trusted historical charity, exploiting a culture of entitlement to steal donated money and use that for personal gain. The next case takes us into a different genre, *key player charity fraud*. The fraud carried out in this genre keeps the focus on corrupt key players in otherwise ethically sound charities. *Key player charity fraud* is what happens when competently managed greed meets incompetently managed audit systems.

Amanda Kate Smith: High-rolling on Public Money

> **ASSOCIATE:** Amanda Kate Smith, you are charged that on diverse dates between the 7th day of May 2008 and the 9th day of May 2015 at the Gold Coast and elsewhere in the State of Queensland, you dishonestly applied to your own use property, namely, bank credits belonging to Smart Employment Solutions Limited, and

you were an employee of Smart Employment Solutions Limited, and the property was of a value of more than $30,000. Amanda Kate Smith, how do you plead: guilty or not guilty?
DEFENDANT: Guilty.
ASSOCIATE: Guilty, Your Honour.
HER HONOUR: Thank you. Call on the defendant.
ASSOCIATE: Amanda Kate Smith, you have been convicted on your own plea of guilty of one count of fraud as an employee to the value of $30,000 or more. Do you have anything to say as to why sentence should not be passed on you?
DEFENDANT: [No][295]

Kate Amanda Smith was an employee of Smart Employment Solutions Limited (SES), a Nerang (Queensland) based registered charity founded in 1986. It describes itself as:

> ... a public benevolent institution in respect of our mission to relieve poverty, distress, misfortune, destitution and helplessness occasioned by unemployment by providing increased education and job opportunities for the unemployed with particular emphasis on youth and the disabled.[296]

Smart Employment Solutions is classed as a large charity. It has 150 paid staff and its gross total income for 2016–17 was $6.7 million.[297]

Smith was employed as a payroll officer responsible for paying the wages of apprentices and trainees, and, most relevantly, remitting tax payments to the ATO. She started offending three years into her employment. Over a seven-year period on one hundred and twenty seven occasions she diverted $1,739,037.12 from two of her employer's bank accounts, meant for payment to ATO, into three bank accounts she controlled.[298] Her fraud was at the high end, given the amount of money she stole and the number of occasions she did so. Her fraudulent modus operandi completely lacked sophistication, a point her defence tried to use to mitigate the sentence. All Smith did was to substitute her own BSB and account details for that of the Australian Taxation Office. Simple as that.

The fraud was finally discovered by the ATO and the charity's chief financial officer, Philip Neale. On the morning of 16 June 2015, Neale spoke to Smith at work to check whether she was following correct banking procedures in processing the tax payments. Smith said she was and denied knowledge of the ANZ account she was depositing the PAYG tax into. By the end of this short interview Smith knew her number was up. She left work, telling colleagues her child was sick. Later that same day Neale reached Smith on her mobile. She repeated her innocence to him, and Neale told her he was calling in the police to identify the mysterious ANZ account. About an hour later Neale received a call from Smith in which she said: "I have been a dishonest employee".[299] When asked by Neale whether there was any money left, Smith said: "No, I've spent it". Prior to this call Smith (who claimed she was now in debt) contacted Queensland Legal Aid who advised her to contact the police and request a notice to appear to avoid her being arrested in front of her child at home.

Smith then sent details of the ANZ account to Neale who contacted the police. They secured all of Smith's accounts and two days later she was interviewed and charged at the Nerang Police Station. When advised of the nature of the complaint the police were pursuing, Smith said:

> I was not in control of what I was doing, and it became an obsession. It consumed me. Then the need to acquire took over my whole life.[300]

Later on in the police interview, Smith said:

> And it's very difficult to explain what went on in my head ... because I can't even explain it to myself. But every time it happened, I would go to myself this will be the last time.

These statements suggest Smith was offering some sort of psychiatric explanation for her behaviour.

When asked what she did with the money Smith said she spent it, "... when we saw something, we bought it". She then corrected herself, "... when I say we I mean me. My husband had no idea". Over a two-year period, Smith purchased three cars and on one occasion she paid for an overseas trip for him that he undertook without her. It is hard to accept that her husband was not complicit.

Smith indicated to the police that, other than the cars, nothing of consequence was purchased with the stolen money. However, police had information that she did spend up big. This included over $30,000 from jewellery stores, over $43,000 from electronics retail stores and $11,000 from toy outlets like Mr. Toys.[301] Smith also withdrew large amounts from ANZ branches and ATM machines, like the withdrawal of $60,000 from the ANZ Branch at Bundall on 7 November 2008.[302]

Smith was aged 28 years at the commencement of the offending and 35 years when her offending was discovered. She presented with no criminal history. At pre-sentence submissions, the DPP said:

> [Kate Amanda Smith] is a mature woman who repeatedly defrauded her employer over an extended period of time. Whilst her deception wasn't particularly sophisticated, she did edit a payment template on each of the 127 occasions to hide the payments which was able to go undetected during internal audits by the company. The maximum penalty ... for this offence was increased from 10 years to 12 years ...[303]

The victim impact statement presented by the charity demonstrated that the consequences had been severe. Whilst the fraud was being committed, the business declined substantially such that the company downsized, even sold assets to keep trading in 2014. The loss to Smart Employment Solutions was in the region of $3.4 million. This is because the ATO has not written off the tax debt. This means Smart Employment Solutions must still pay this debt twice. For some time, the charity swayed on the brink of liquidation.

Smith told police she was "flabbergasted" that she was not caught. SES employed three different auditors throughout the long offending period and none of them picked up the fraud. Evidence was given at the trial that the three auditors had unimpeded access to SES's financial records. SES'S audit procedures were, to be blunt, bungling and inept. A similar criticism can be made of the audit efficiency of the Australian Taxation Office. For seven years, it did not notice that SES was not forwarding on PAYG payments.

Smith was made redundant in 2014 due to deteriorating business conditions that she caused. At that point Smith had taken $1.46 million from the charity. She must have been very surprised when the charity, still unaware of her stealing, subsequently rehired her on a contract basis to fill a maternity leave position. Back in the job, Smith took another $270,790 out of the charity before she was finally exposed.

When she was interviewed by police in June 2015, Smith made certain admissions that seemed to imply that she had lost control over her stealing.[304] However she contradicted this later in the interview when she seemed aware enough of her actions to suggest that each time she made the illegal transfer it would be the last time that she would do so. Whatever credence one gives to these excuses, it is clear that Smith was funding a lifestyle for herself and her family and she was never going to give up.

At her trial the Director of Public Prosecutions said:

> In my submission, the fraud is one based on greed, not need ... the moneys obtained were spent on new cars, holidays, buying goods at retail stores and electronics stores and jewellery, amongst other items ... [including the purchase of] three special interest military vehicles by the defendant's husband. An analysis of the funds spent on jewellery, retail stores, baby stores and tattoo studios accounts for just over $124,000 during the period.[305]

Although the DPP did not produce any evidence to the point, he suggested to the court that Smith still had most of the stolen money in a secret place:

> ... it would seem that [there is] ... somewhere in the region of $1.4 million still unaccounted for. ... Ms Smith has not made any efforts of restitution to date and appears to maintain that all of the money obtained unlawfully has been spent and that she is now in debt.[306]

The possibility that Smith was hoarding her illicit gains for enjoyment once she left prison was also considered by Professor Ashley Goldsworthy, the CEO of SES, in the victim impact statement tendered to the court.[307]

For six years Amanda Kate Smith defrauded the Commonwealth of $1.7 million in lost tax revenue. Six years of audits, six years in which no red lights flashed at ATO that it was not getting the required PAYG income from Smart Employment Solutions, six years in which the charity did not smell a rat, despite having some financial whizzes on the Board. Amanda Kate Smith merely stumbled onto an interlocked checks and balances regime both within and outside the charity that was, simply put, asleep.

In our journey through the land of giving so far, the case material has shown three faces of charity wrongdoing. The Shane Warne Foundation case was a clear exemplar of flaws in the increasingly popular celebrity charity model. The charity regulator, ACNC, took away the Foundation's operating licence, not for proven fraud but for failing to return adequate levels of donations to the nominated beneficiaries.

The celebrity charity model, in its most repugnant iteration, is one that knows the world of money and how to make it quickly for a select few beneficiary charities. This is achieved through glitzy star-studded events, usually for the high end of town. Money collected from these events is then passed to worthwhile but "safe" (read non-controversial) charities such as the Starlight Foundation and Clown Doctors. It is highly unlikely that money raised through celebrity charities would ever endow high risk or start up experimental charities. Nor would it endow socially marginal projects such as art classes in maximum security prisons. In the sick, hidden logic of the celebrity charity model, the chosen beneficiary must also bring star value to the donors.

The celebrity charity model is a perfect vehicle for party goers. You get heaps of good publicity, have a fun time and don't have to think too hard about the big social issues like poverty. Of the charity models considered here, the celebrity model is the one most exposed to tokenism, and worse, hypocrisy.

We are reminded of these elements each year at the annual fund raiser for the homeless sponsored by the St. Vincent de Paul Society. The site of bleary-eyed CEOs emerging from their night of "sleeping rough" and fumbling for their keys to their BMWs to transport them back to the land of privilege, leaves many people shaking their heads at the tokenism and hypocrisy that can be embedded in this donation model.

Just when we thought this donation model could not be any more morally repugnant, along comes the Logie winning 2017 SBS documentary, *Filthy Rich and Homeless*. A more morally depraved version of "I'm a celebrity, get me out of here", it follows five people who are given a ten-day taste of homelessness. The production was a great success. SBS made heaps of money, the participants had their profiles glistened and the voyeuristic viewing public got some forgettable raw vision.[308]

So successful was the documentary that SBS aired the second series with another five luxury homeowners in August 2018. The second series was supported by around $300,000 taxpayer dollars from Screen Australia, a Commonwealth Government Agency.[309] In an irony that can be nothing short of tragic, this Commonwealth funding was about the same as the annual Commonwealth funding for Homelessness Australia (HA), an important conduit between government and frontline services that provided research and capacity-building. Important that is until it was axed in December 2014 and the money returned to government savings.[310] So the government is funding an SBS documentary about what happens to homeless people when the government does not fund the critical services!

The story gets a little bit more distasteful still. To manipulate the viewing audiences that SBS was really doing something for the homeless it entered into an arrangement with Foodora, a German start up that delivered online ordered meals into a $20 billion market. For every meal delivered Foodora asked customers to donate a meal for the homeless through Oz Harvest.[311] SBS could have done a little bit more due diligence in relation to this business partnership. In June 2018, the Fair Work Ombudsman filed a legally significant action in the Federal Court, accusing the organisation of entering into sham contracts with its drivers. On 20 August 2018, Foodora closed and left Australia, saying it was not making enough money here.[312]

The RSL case followed. It explained how venerability is no longer a foil for historical charities that fall into deep legal and moral error. The case mapped the spiralling RSL greed culture and how it has been incubated in the sometimes cosy, sometimes cranky interpersonal relationships of the power group. These donation-stealing ex-diggers felt a level of personal entitlement and self-giving because of war service and post-war volunteer work that the community is no longer prepared to grant as a reason to diminish culpability for charity fraud.

The RSL case also allowed us to consider the contradictory winds buffeting large charities: when mission meets money, to put it succinctly. On one hand there is the original purpose to operate for charitable purposes. On the other hand, when a charity becomes a mega business like the RSL, it must sail with the winds of financial efficiency, infrastructure accumulation and (controversially) profit management. The standard bearer for this is the RSL owned four-star, ninety seven room hotel in the middle of the Sydney CBD, Hyde Park Inn, at 271 Elizabeth Street, an asset worth in excess of $90 million.[313] The question should be written in the sky: what is a charity doing with so much wealth? With this much affluence one wonders why the RSL continues to be a registered charity, and why it is continually seeking government grants and tax-free donations from a hard-pressed donor community.

The final short case, illustrating a specific charity fraud genre, was that of Amanda Kate Smith. This genre, the simplest of all, is, as noted, called key player charity fraud. It's the simplest of all because there are very few moving parts. Usually it's just two: a strategically placed charity worker with criminal intent in an accounting system that is either incompetently devised or incompetently managed.

Now, onto the final case, that of Eman Sharobeem at the Immigrant Women's Health Service (IWHS). It was a damning investigation by the NSW Independent Commission against Corruption (ICAC).

Chapter Five
The Corruption of Eman Sharobeem

Ms Sharobeem's evidence was often inconsistent, ambiguous and contradictory.

Reginald Blanch QC, ICAC Commissioner

Two photographs bookend the corrupt career of Eman Sharobeem. In the first she is glowing. Former NSW Premier, Mike Baird, is presenting her with her nomination for the 2015 Australian of the Year. In the second photograph, taken two years later, she is gaunt, grey-faced and scarred. She is walking with her legal team into the fateful ICAC hearing, gripping a luxury handbag and wearing a fixed smile. Her fall, Icarus-like, was now complete.

As a result of more than two thousand transcript pages and numerous exhibits, the ICAC hearing into Eman Sharobeem's offending offers an abundance of insights into the fine details and hidden nuances of charity fraud.

My first section, "Her Early Story", is a short biographical note which sees Sharobeem's move from a middle-class upbringing in Cairo to the western Sydney suburb of Parramatta, then, mysteriously, back to Egypt where she apparently had senior foreign aid jobs. Equally puzzling, Sharobeem then returned to Sydney and began her fatal involvement with two charities: the Immigrant Women's Health Service and the Non-English-Speaking Housing Women's Scheme. She would ultimately destroy these two well intentioned organisations through her unrestrained greed and narcissism.

Following this, in "Celebrity Advocate and Big Spender", her secret double life is exposed. This is done in the same way she lived her life. She blended her public persona (media darling, apex role model for immigrant women, welfare socialite) with her high-living private life that was funded through the wanton pillaging of public money earmarked for worthy charitable purposes.

By this stage of the narrative the curiosity about her psychology is overwhelming. It is explored in "Personality of a Fraudster". In the absence of a full confession from Sharobeem, this section remains speculative with a profusion of questions and very few answers. Did she turn from a life of good intention to a life of bad intention suddenly? If so, what were the triggers? Are they to be found in her culture, her family or her own immigrant status? Or, was the good-intentioned life a cover for a woman who from the start cared nothing about suffering in the human condition? The best speculation we can arrive at from the available evidence is that she was driven by monumental greed and a cold nonchalance bordering on wilful disregard about the plight of immigrant women, many of whom were refugees from some of the world's most terrifying hotspots. That both the charities she destroyed could have done so much for these women adds another layer onto this tragedy.

The question: "How did she get away with it for so long?" is explored in "Two Zombie Boards, Two Broken Charities", an analysis of the boards that were supposed to be governing the two charities. They protected Sharobeem until it became impossible to do so any longer.

"The Slow Downfall" documents her last days in office. A combination of official snail-pacing matched with a reluctance to believe she was capable of criminal acts, ensured that her toppling happened in slow motion.

While her primary motivations remain blurred, we examine how Sharobeem conducted herself under investigation in "Lies and Moral Indignation. Weapons of Choice for the Trapped". Finally, "Eman Sharobeem: Her Date with Justice" details the legal proceedings against her, specifically the damning findings.

Before we move forward, a note of caution. The ICAC investigation took exhaustive oral evidence from Sharobeem over nine days. It concluded:

> Ms Sharobeem's evidence was often inconsistent, ambiguous and contradictory. On issues of substance, her evidence often deviated

from objectively established facts. Such matters call into question her credibility. The Commission therefore came to the view that it could not accept her evidence on any contentious issue unless it involved an admission against interest or was corroborated by other reliable evidence.[314]

The following account proceeds on the same basis.

Her Early Story

Eman Sharobeem was born in Cairo, Egypt, on 3 June 1963, into a professional family of the Coptic faith. Her father and mother were both in the Education Department, and her father, Addly, rose to be Principal of a school. Sharobeem would later claim that she came to Australia in 1977 as a fourteen-year-old and was forcibly married as a child bride in 1978, when she was 15 years old. This lie was exposed by the *Sydney Morning Herald* in 2017.

In 1984 she married for the first time when she was twenty one.[315] She and her husband, Gamelshawky Sharobeem, met while students at Ain Shams University in Cairo.[316] She would later claim that he developed schizophrenia and raped her in the marriage.[317] On 1 April 1987 she and her husband came to Australia and settled in Parramatta.[318] The following year her first child, Charlie, was born. Charlie would figure prominently in his mother's corrupt behaviour. From that year, until 1991, Sharobeem worked first as a liaison officer at Doonside High School and then as a welfare worker with the Granville Multicultural Centre, although there is no evidence that she had formal social work qualifications.[319] In 1992, her second child, Richard, who would also join his mother's corrupt team, was born. Two years later she started (but apparently did not finish) a Diploma of Community Studies at the University of Technology Sydney (UTS).[320] Sharobeem would, years later, repeatedly lie about her UTS qualifications.

In 1995, she returned briefly to Egypt, and again in 1997. Her explanation, that she went back to Egypt in 1997 to have her sons Charlie (then 9 years old) and Richard (then 5 years old) baptised, does not stack up.[321] She also gave evidence that the local Coptic priest in Fairfield was so distressed at her treatment by her husband, Gamel, that he bought airline tickets for her and children to travel to Cairo. She said that Gamel followed her, seized her passport and absconded with the children for 55 days.[322]

In July 1997, while living in a posh part of Nasr City, Egypt, Sharobeem was appointed Executive Director of the Micro Enterprise Unit in the Giza Governorate. This was a development partnership program with the Italian Government.[323] This position lasted until December 1999. With a very complimentary reference from her manager, who said "her honesty ... make(s) her a valuable asset to any organisation ..." Sharobeem then joined the Institute of International Education, an American development initiative in Giza. A year later she was able to secure another glowing reference, this time from Melanie Sanders-Smith, Chief of Party (USAID-Institute of International Education).[324]

In 2002, she claimed to have received an honorary degree from the American University in Cairo.[325] When this claim was closely examined years later, it turned out to be false. Is it just coincidental that her mentor, Suzanne Mubarack, the wife of the deposed Egyptian dictator, had received an honorary doctorate from the same University two years earlier? It does look like Sharobeem enmeshed herself quickly into a web of high-level patronage that remains inscrutable to the outside observer.

Sharobeem then moved onto the Egyptian National Council of Women, as General Director, External Relations Department, in 2002. It was around this time Sharobeem started to refer to herself as "Doctor". This act of deception with regards to her having a doctorate, is the earliest clear evidence we have of her compromised moral character.

Again, this deceptive act is hard to decipher. Is it possible she felt she needed an overlay of false credentialing to impress her rich and powerful patrons? Whether this was the start of her ethical waywardness or not, one thing is certain: her compromised moral character would make a huge negative impact on the immigrant social services scene in western Sydney when she returned. What makes Sharobeem's insinuation into the centre of government and diplomatic circles even more extraordinary is that she came from a Coptic background. She returned to an Egypt that was making it hard for the Coptic minority.[326] It would have been a tricky manoeuvre for her and she must have had extremely good contacts and have known how to use them. She was operating in a world of corrupt Egyptian officials, most of whom were men. Her attractive looks and her vivaciousness were well appreciated.

On 25 March 2002, there was an invitation to "Dr. Imane Charobine, Egypt" from the World Bank Centre for Arab Women for Training and Research, for a day seminar and briefing.[327] In February 2003 she received an invitation from the Spanish Ambassador to Egypt to brief him in his Cairo Embassy, prior to the arrival in Cairo of a delegation from the Spanish Agency for International Cooperation.[328] She was mixing in high status circles in Cairo and Giza. She claimed she was a women's advocate working for Suzanne Mubarak, and later with Queen Rania of Jordan.[329] Suzanne Mubarak was the first head of the state-controlled National Council of Women where Sharobeem worked for over two years, so that claim was probably correct.

Circling in Suzanne Mubarak's orbit of influence for over two years would not have been without its consequences for Sharobeem's moral development. Suzanne Mubarak had been first lady of Egypt for twenty one years when Sharobeem joined her at the National Council of Women. Suzanne Mubarak was to Egypt what Imelda Marcos was to the Philippines: a figure of hate who ruled behind a weak husband. She was corrupt, arrogant and one who showed callous disregard for the poor. As one commentator has said, Suzanne Mubarak "observed Cairo's garbage-strewn streets through a gilded peephole".[330] As Suzanne Mubarak sequestered billions of Egyptian pounds in overseas banks, she maintained a public persona of public service for which her obsequious admirers would shower her with awards and recognitions. When asked what the most important thing to Suzanne Mubarak was, Farouk Hosny, the former Minister for Culture said, "To win an international prize". Many Egyptians whispered that she dreamed of a Nobel Prize.[331] This lady was Sharobeem's moral mentor.

As we go further into Sharobeem's story, the equivalence between her resumé and that of Suzanne Mubarak will be striking. Both women had unquestioned matriarchal power and surrounded themselves with weak, greedy men. Both women made corruption a family affair. Both women craved for public recognition. Both women had no impact on advancing the welfare of those groups they advocated for. Both women were deluded about the possibility of State retaliation for their crimes and both women had their assets frozen by their respective governments. We simply cannot ignore that 2002–2003 period in Sharobeem's life when she entered Suzanne Mubarak's sphere of influence. Back in Sydney some years later, Sharobeem, on a smaller scale, would also pillage the public purse and lust over awards and commendations.

In September 2003, Sharobeem resigned from National Council of Women, and with another career-boosting reference from a life-long friend of Suzanne Mubarak, Farkhonda Hassan, Secretary-General of the National Council of Women, Sharobeem inexplicably returned to Australia. Is it possible that she re-migrated to Australia to avoid some formal investigation into her behaviour by Egyptian authorities? Whatever, but we can be sure that by the time she was back in Sydney her Mubarak-mentored apprenticeship was complete. From day one she did nothing without an eye to beguiling the media. She was comfortable with power and mixed easily in Sydney political circles. Her taste for the good things in life sat paradoxically with her complete indifference to the suffering of others, especially Middle Eastern women refugees and migrants.

It seems that she quickly found re-employment with IWHS as project coordinator at the Cabramatta branch. Very soon, in August 2004, she was promoted to IWHS manager and worked from the organisation's head office at 92 Smart Street Fairfield. In an extraordinary act of criminal audaciousness Sharobeem would secretly buy this property and lease it back to IWHS at a grossly inflated rent.

Sometime later, in 2006, Sharobeem informed her staff at IWHS that she had completed a degree and was now a practising psychologist. She referred to herself as "Dr Sharobeem" and expected others to do the same. Confoundingly, Sharobeem started to apply for welfare jobs which appeared to be below the level of IWHS manager. In January 2007, she applied for positions with NSW TAFE and the Smith Family. On both occasions she used false qualifications.[332] In January 2008, Sharobeem made her first recorded improper use of her IWHS credit card.[333] Her fraudulent behaviour would continue for eight years until she resigned in January 2016.

Celebrity Advocate and Big Spender

In this section, Sharobeem's welfare advocacy for immigrant women and her extensive illegal spending are laid side by side. One fed the other. The more she became a media celebrity and member of high-powered commissions the more she was emboldened to misspend taxpayer's money. Suzanne Mubarak would have been proud.

By early 2011, Sharobeem's fortunes were running high. In February she successfully applied for a part-time position with the NSW Community Relations Commission (now Multicultural NSW). This appointment was the perfect cover for her corrupt behaviour. It had her out and about in the migrant community talking it up to an increasingly credulous and admiring audience. One of her referees for the NSW Community Relations Commission position was Naguib "Nick" Kaldas, who in the same year, 2011, became the Deputy Commissioner of the New South Wales Police. Like Sharobeem, Kaldas was a Coptic Egyptian. Her time on the Community Relations Commission was to last from 2011 to 2016. In that period, she received approximately $15,000 in remuneration from the Community Relations Commission. In her application for this position she replaced her bogus American University of Cairo PhD with an equally bogus PhD from the University of Technology Sydney. No one checked this, or the spelling and grammar mistakes strewn across her application.

She received notice of her successful appointment to the Community Relations Commission in March 2011. Perhaps wishing to celebrate, Sharobeem went on a personal shopping spree with taxpayers' money in her purse. She developed two ruses to hide this spending. She would buy something for herself or family usually with her own credit card. Then she would cut off the receipt details of the items purchased and submit the receipt for payment with a statement that the item was for IWHS or NESH. The other way was to seek reimbursement without supporting evidence for non-existent goods and services, which she said were purchased for IWHS or NESH but were always delivered to her residence. In the four months after her appointment to the Community Relations Commission she bought for herself: a Breville slow cooker ($115), a Breville juice maker ($140), a $135

Swatch watch and a $159 Olympus camera. In addition, she got reimbursed for ghost goods and services such as $3100 for a wardrobe that was never purchased, $860 for the repair of the gate at IWHS that was never fixed and $13,000 for a pour of concrete in the front of IWHS that never occurred.

In September 2011, Sharobeem represented the Community Relations Commission Chair at a function marking the 10th Anniversary of the Multicultural Problem Gambling Service NSW. Two days later she was representing the Commission Chair again at an anniversary ball for Handital NSW INC, an Italian community-based advocacy and support service for people with disabilities. Two weeks later she was out spending taxpayer money. This time for $795 worth of white goods from the major home merchandise group, Bing Lee. In fact, the ICAC forensic investigation found that from this first purchase until January 2015 Sharobeem bought $7785 worth of personal items from Bing Lee alone and charged them all to the IWHS account.[334]

In April 2012, Sharobeem was out and about again. This time at a Corporate Club Australia Networking Breakfast at the Museum of Contemporary Art in Sydney. She attended this function in her capacity as a Commissioner with the Community Relations Commission. Perhaps feeling the pressures of work, a fortnight later she paid $8900 from IWHS funds for a family membership with the timeshare holiday company, Classic Holidays Club. She was now at the stage of feeling bullet-proof. One can see that clearly in the reckless invoice she sent through to IWHS for the payment for a non-existent "handyman" to facilitate a support group for Middle Eastern women.[335] It really challenges the imagination to understand how these outrageous payments could be believed let alone paid. As we will see further on, the often less well-educated, deferential, Middle Eastern women who staffed the centres she controlled were no match for Sharobeem's star quality, the way she dressed, the way she talked, the way she was always being interviewed or quoted.

On 29 May 2012, she was a guest on the SBS program, *Insight,* which considered polygamy in Australia. SBS described her as a psychologist who believed religion can subjugate women into accepting polygamous relationships.[336] By now Sharobeem was the migrant women's success story. The story was still five years away from being exposed as a list of lies. For now, she was the child bride from Egypt who found her voice in Australia and was using that voice, she said, to empower other migrant women.

A week after her appearance on *Insight* she was representing the Chair of the Community Relations Commission at the opening night of the Sydney Film Festival. It is possible she wore the expensive Ponti dress to that occasion that she had purchased four days before and billed the taxpayer.

On 23 June 2012, Sharobeem was again representing the Community Relations Commission Chair, this time at a Horn of Africa cultural night put on by the Horn of Africa Relief and Development Agency. What she did just before that defies belief: prior to attending and being seen to support action in one of the most troubled regions of the world, Sharobeem had for most of that month been submitting invoices for cleaning the IWHS centre in Fairfield. The cleaning services were fakes and the name she used on the invoices, "Rachel Kamol", was also fake. For example, on the invoice for 19 June 2012, she claimed $57 for cleaning the Fairfield centre and $150 for assembling a non-existent chair. The ICAC evidence was that neither of these maintenance actions occurred.

The facts that are emerging in this story about her spending, big and small (such as those bogus $57 cleaning charges) direct us to a woman who was completely out of moral control. She was taking every opportunity to suck both her organisations (IWHS and NESH) dry, with no guilt, no remorse. The massive fraud she committed actually defunded services for, ironically, women like herself of recent immigrant background: immigrants and refugees who sought help from IWHS and NESH because they were struggling with huge social, economic and cultural adjustments. She was literally taking bread out of their mouths. Her industrial scale greed explains a lot of her motivation, but not everything.

Maybe the poor female immigrants and refugees she encountered at work elicited a sense of repugnance in her. Maybe they reminded her of who she was, or who she might have been, and she wished to close that memory down as she was now not one of them. She was now a star, living in a big house with a husband driving around in a Mercedes (which she paid for with IWHS funds). We will try and pick up more of the scent on this trail as we go further into her story. We will also have to address another question now emerging in the account. Why were all these dodgy invoices getting through? That question will be considered when Sharobeem's work culture is analysed below. But for now, we continue examining her work activities in juxtaposition to her misspending.

On 19 July, a month after she claimed $57 for not cleaning the Fairfield centre and $150 for not assembling a non-existent chair, "Rachel Kamol" presented another false invoice for $57 for "cleaning" the Fairfield office from 4–7pm. Did she have time to go home and clean up or did she go straight to Parramatta Myers where she purchased a $129 Breville safety urn at 8.09pm and a $140 Volta vacuum cleaner at 8.16pm?[337] Two days later she represented the Community Relations Commission Chair at a function at the Mandaean Australian Community Cultural Club, to help celebrate Mandaean New Year.

By now the darling of SBS and ABC, Sharobeem (ES) was interviewed by the well-respected, but on this occasion gullible, Rachael Kohn (RK), on the *The Spirit of Things* on 29 July.[338]

> **RK:** Dr Eman Sharobeem, welcome to *The Spirit of Things*.
> **ES:** Thank you for having me Rachael.
> **RK:** You have brought the subject of forced marriage out into the open recently in an article that appeared in *The Australian Magazine*, and since you have experienced it yourself to some extent you're in a good position to know how it all happens.

Rachael Kohn then led Sharobeem into what we now know was a fictionalised account of her forced marriage at 14. The interview progresses to the time she came to Australia with her husband.

> **RK:** Well you got married and you came to Australia, but your husband became ill and you were widowed at 29. What did you feel like then?
> ...
> **ES:** I knew of his illness and that he suffered a couple of nervous breakdowns before and he is on medication. So basically, I stayed and lived with him for 10 years while I lived with a sick man ... Where I am now as a Doctor of Psychology started because of him. It was my intention as a devoted wife to study what is happening with him, to know and to learn how to deal with him. So, every

> time I started to learn something I gained another certificate, and on my graduation, I actually dedicated my PhD to him, and said that without my extremely violent and ill man, I wouldn't be where I am.
>
> ...
>
> **RK:** So you had actually been forced into a marriage that ended up being quite dangerous for you?
>
> **ES:** Very much so, and everyone in the marriage was devastated to know that I hid all this information for many years.

A week after this interview Sharobeem billed IWHS for $2000 in cosmetic care and products at the Lily Room, and for the rest of 2012 made a further twenty eight false claims for office cleaning under the name Rachel Kamol. Her Christmas shopping that year included a $499 Dyson vacuum cleaner and a $95 Morphy toaster, courtesy again of the Australian taxpayer.

Things continued in this fashion throughout 2013: glitzy events, media interviews ... and stealing. In February 2013, Sharobeem attended the thirtieth anniversary of the Muslim Women's Association. Straight away after that event she and her family travelled to the Pacific Palms Resort at Surfers Paradise for one of her Classic Holiday Club bookings, all paid for by the taxpayer. She returned to receive, in March, an inaugural Australian Arab Women's Award for unwavering leadership in the field of migrant women's welfare.

In April 2013, she made the first illegal payment to the Bonnyrigg Garden Centre for various items to adorn the garden at her house. Evidence to the *Operation Tarlo* hearing showed that between April 2013 and March 2015 Sharobeem illegally purchased $5428 worth of items from that garden centre.[339] Some of these items were found when ICAC raided her house.

For the rest of 2013, in a parallel universe, where adulation not the truth is the default position, her star continued to rise. In August, she claimed another victim when her local member, Gaetano ("Guy") Zangari, moved a commendation for her work in the New South Wales Legislative Assembly:

> I congratulate Dr Eman Sharobeem on her commitment to supporting refugees, asylum seekers and migrants. Dr Sharobeem's work was recognised – and rightly so – by her being

named a finalist at the 2013 Women of the Year Awards by the Department of Family and Community Services.[340]

She was like a child in a chocolate factory. There was no end to her appetite for glory. In September 2013, obviously underqualified, she audaciously applied for the position of Chairperson of the Community Relations Commission. Again, she cited her false PhD. She was unsuccessful.

In the same month, Sharobeem proposed a memorandum of understanding to combine NESH and IWHS into Immigration and Refugee Women's Services NSW, with her as overall CEO. While there may have been good administrative reasons why IWHS and NESH should merge, they are illusive. It appears as a power grab. The ensuing ICAC investigation heard evidence that some Board members knew nothing about the proposal.[341] The merger was confirmed on 12 December with a function at NSW Parliament House. On 28 December, Sharobeem checked into the Surfers Royal Resort to spend some more taxpayer's money.

In 2014, for unknown reasons, Sharobeem changed her petty crime tactics. Instead of submitting numerous false office cleaning claims, she now started to submit facilitator claims for running groups that never existed. Throughout 2014, using false names such as "Emma Adly" and "Rachel Kamol", Sharobeem submitted forty nine false claims for facilitation work when there is no evidence she ran any groups at all. At the height of her powers, and with no one in the office daring to resist her or ask questions about the claims, all payment submissions went through.

What is so striking about these claims is that even the most casual glance at them would have seen how utterly preposterous they were. Just a few examples will suffice here. Sharobeem submitted a claim for doing facilitator work on 25 January, the day she was in Canberra attending an Australia Day function.[342] She submitted a facilitation claim for 14 February, when phone records show she was at a Community Relations Commission meeting that day.[343] She claimed facilitation hours for 19 April, a day she was many miles away, on holidays in Fingal Bay. Her best work was yet to come. On 23 and 24 May, under the alias, "Emma Adly", Sharobeem submitted false facilitation claims *four times* for the same hours worked!

June was a particularly lucrative month for Sharobeem. It started with a $975 reimbursement for cosmetic care at the Lily Room. This was around the time her son Richard, using the false name "Rachie Kakal", was paid $900 for facilitation work that never happened.[344] Like mother, like son. Richard had no training whatsoever to perform the tasks of a facilitator. On 8 June, Sharobeem purchased a 630 litre fridge for her house for $4000. The first two attempts to pay for the fridge with her Visa card failed. The payment was accepted on the third occasion using her Mastercard. Sharobeem then submitted for payment the two declined Visa card receipts along with the accepted Mastercard receipt! She ended up getting a new fridge and a $12,000 consolation prize.[345] Four days before an IWHS Board meeting on 12 June, again with public funds earmarked for migrant women's welfare, Sharobeem purchased an 18ct white gold diamond necklace plus two studs for $20,000.[346] The minutes of the Board meeting that followed this purchase were uneventful. Board behaviour will be analysed shortly. Suffice to say that Sharobeem kept these meetings uneventful by depriving the Board of the necessary information it needed to perform its role to the regulator's expectation.

A fortnight before, she used public money to pay for her Botox treatment worth just under $1000 from the Lily Room.[347] She was certainly looking better than the financial accounts back at IWHS and NESH. Now, for the first time, someone started to query what Sharobeem was up to. This was IWHS's indefatigable auditor, Nathan Boyd. Unaware that Sharobeem was using aliases, Boyd sent an Audit Management Letter to the Board regarding double payments to some facilitators.[348] The Board never got this letter because Sharobeem got to it first. Boyd would weather much denial and obfuscation from Sharobeem as he moved forward to eventually provide an adverse audit.

The year finished with the usual mix of media adulation, gushing testimonials from politicians and grand scale theft. On 5 November, the Hon. Marie Ficarra of the NSW Legislative Council, moved the following motion. It is recorded here in its completeness because if offers a neat appraisal of how Sharobeem was officially viewed at the time:

1. That this House notes:
a. The outstanding work of Dr Eman Sharobeem for almost three decades for immigrant and refugee communities in Australia and abroad, especially for women and their families;
b. That Dr Eman Sharobeem's hard work and commitment has helped shape the global paradigm shift on policies and programs impacting the lives of tens of thousands of women and has promoted a greater gender equality whilst simultaneously stimulating greater public awareness and community harmony;
c. That at the present time Dr Eman Sharobeem is a serving member of numerous organisations representing immigrant and refugee women, including:
   i. The Chief Executive Officer of Immigrant Women's Health Service;
   ii. A statutory Board member of the Anti-Discrimination Board, NSW;
   iii. Advisory Board member of the Community Relations Commission for Multicultural NSW;
   iv. Convenor of the Immigrant and Refugee Women's network;
   v. Chairwoman of Non-English-Speaking Housing;
   vi. Member of the Association of Former International Civil Servants;
   vii. Member of the NSW Domestic and Family Violence Council;
d. That Dr Eman Sharobeem has received many accolades in recognition of her outstanding contribution to improving the lives of many immigrant and refugee women, including:
   i. The Ambassador for India Australia Business and Community Award in 2014;
   ii. The Australian Egyptian of the Year in 2014;
   iii. A certificate of commendation from the Parliament of Australia in recognition of her service and inspiration to Australian women;
   iv. An Australia Day Ambassador in 2014; and
   v. Being selected as a finalist in the Premier's Award for Women in 2013;
e. That apart from Dr Eman Sharobeem's active service to the immigrant and refugee community within Australia, she has also served actively abroad, including:

i. Serving as a manager of the Micro Finance Unit for the United Nations taskforce in Egypt;
ii. Serving as a mediator and negotiator of USAID Education Treaties with the Middle East in Egypt, Jordan and Tunisia; and
iii. Serving as the General Manager of the Department of International Relations of the National Council of Women in Egypt;

f. That one of Dr Eman Sharobeem's greatest contributions in Australia is exemplified through her involvement in the Immigrant Women's Health Service, which promotes the physical, emotional and psychological wellbeing of women in immigrant and refugee communities in order for them to be able to lead healthy, fulfilling lives in Australia;
g. That the service is staffed by 23 part-time workers and 35 volunteers who run social support groups, literacy programs and health information workshops; and
h. That between 2013 and 2014, the Immigrant Women's Health Service attended to 12,201 cases [*sic*] on a variety of matters including: violence, child marriage, drug and gambling addictions, female genital mutilation, through to learning English and understanding life in Australia.

2. That this House:

a. Commends Dr Eman Sharobeem on her many years of outstanding service to the tens of thousands of women and their families living in immigrant and refugee communities both in Australia and throughout the world;
b. Recognises the importance of organisations such as the Immigrant Women's Health Service in delivering partnership programs between various ethnic communities and promoting multiculturalism and integration in New South Wales, where there are large ethnic immigrant and refugee communities; and
c. Wishes Dr Eman Sharobeem all the very best in her future endeavours.

Ficarra's dry run for a Noble Peace Prize nomination for Sharobeem was soon followed in December by more fawning media attention.

The highly respected Richard Aedy fell for her allure and had Sharobeem on his *Sunday Profile* interview, on ABC Radio.[349] Aedy introduced Sharobeem by recycling her lie that she was forced into a marriage at fifteen years of age. She was allowed to grandstand herself when she talked of the threats she had received:

> Actually, one of them said be careful – you might be beheaded next. But did I stop? No. Am I going to? No. Would that make me afraid? No. Because what I say is for the benefit of all our communities.

With money that should have gone to the places Ficarra gushed about, Sharobeem went out and bought a Honda City car for the exclusive use of her two sons Charlie and Richard and a $35,000 Mercedes 300B for her second husband, Haimon Hammo.[350]

IWHS was established in 1987, seventeen years before Sharobeem came on the scene in 2004. The service provided free educational, recreational and developmental programs for immigrant and refugee women from what was referred to as culturally and linguistically diverse backgrounds (CALD). The service was primarily funded by the Southwest Sydney Local Health District of the New South Wales Department of Health.

The sister charity, the Non-English-Speaking Housing Women's Scheme Inc. was funded by the New South Wales Department of Family and Community Services through the Supported Accommodation Assistance Program. Houses were provided by the Department to NESH in the Liverpool and Fairfield areas. NESH would then place migrant women and children into these places according to need for up to one year.

Both agencies were governed by boards. Did they govern effectively and keep Sharobeem accountable? The unequivocal answer is no.

Personality of a Fraudster

Various staff gave evidence at the ICAC hearing about Eman Sharobeem's personality and leadership style. One was Marie Abboud, the IWHS administrator for five years, as well as facilitator for Arabic women's groups:

> When I first met Eman, she was a very calm person towards other people. We thought she was godsend as she was very supportive, very kind, very nice and was trying to make us happy and give us work ... I thought back in the early days, 'my god this woman is so

good' but I later realised that it was all for her own benefit because she knew that I could handle the place on my own without her being there which I did. Everyone knew that I was underpaid the whole time I was working there. People would tell me to go and do something about it but I just said, "It's okay. I'm not here for the money." I think Eman took this for granted and took advantage of me.[351]

Abboud said that Sharobeem never bought gifts for staff, nor honoured their birthdays. She noticed that Sharobeem's leadership style had become authoritarian:

> Eman was initially very nice but we later saw the other side of her. By that I mean that she wasn't as kind as she used to be. She wasn't asking us to do things, she was telling us, ordering us. She had become more powerful and if there was something that she told me to do that I wasn't happy about, she would just look at me in a certain way and give me a look, suggesting that I just had to do it.[352]

Soon Sharobeem's behaviour engendered a deep distrust among the workers:

> There were times when I recall Eman would have some appointments for the day and she would say to me, "I've gone to be at a meeting. I won't be back until later so cancel these appointments for today." She would come back with her hair done, nails done and I could tell that she hadn't been to a meeting, she had been to the hairdressers and nail clinic. I used to think to myself, 'why is she lying? Why would she say she is in a meeting when she is getting her hair done?'[353]

Sharobeem started at IWHS in 2004. Between then and 2008 there is no evidence of wrongdoing at all. Four years of reasonable behaviour and then a quick spiral into wrongdoing. Marie Abboud, the IWHS administrator gave evidence on this:

> Eman has shown a difference in her appearance since she first started at IWHS. Probably about 4 years after she started her clothes and her appearance changed a lot. She started to dress really nicely with her hair and nails always done and wearing nice jewellery as well.

This fashion makeover was accompanied by a change in behaviour. Sharobeem was becoming bossier. Marie Abboud again:

> I never spoke to Eman about these issues with the facilitators as she wouldn't let people speak about anything. I didn't feel as though I could have confronted her with any of this and if I had I believe the outcome would have been very bad.[354]

When asked for his opinion on Sharobeem's style, Nathan Boyd, the charity's accountant said: "I would describe Eman as a very dominant person by nature. I think that whatever Eman decided, everyone around her would simply have to agree with her".[355] Similar evidence was obtained from the harried IWHS and NESH bookkeeper, Chanthaneth Chanthalangsy ("Neth"):

> **ICAC:** So would you agree that she would tell you abruptly to do what you were told?
> **CHANTHALANGSY:** Yes.
> **ICAC:** Quickly?
> **CHANTHALANGSY:** That's like when people ask question too much.
> **ICAC:** Do you think she would get frustrated when you asked her questions about the reimbursements?
> **CHANTHALANGSY:** Angry.
> **ICAC:** She would get angry?
> **CHANTHALANGSY:** Yes, when you ask.[356]

Watfa El-Bal recalled in her statement the importance that Sharobeem was placing on her emerging media profile:

> I recall asking her once why she did not display her qualifications and her response was because she did not want to show off. This comment was strange as she is always in the newspapers and couldn't wait to show us the latest photo of her in the magazine or newspaper. Therefore, whenever she had any article or photos of hers in any newspaper she would ask me or Marie to enlarge it, laminate it then hang it in the hallway wall.[357]

Sharobeem was not playing it fair by the staff. Nevine Ghaly, one of the workers who eventually came forward, said in evidence:

> I looked up to Eman because of the work that she was doing. Sometimes, I didn't understand the work but I knew that she was

a high profile person and I thought I could assist her. I liked to assist people and sort of stay in the background myself. Over time working in that office, I realised that Eman wasn't the person that I thought she was, particularly in terms of how she conducted herself with the staff. By that I mean that I found out by talking to other staff that Eman would set people up against each other and we all soon discovered this. I found that Eman wasn't the person that she portrayed herself to be. She portrayed herself to be a person of high character and standards who was a humanitarian but I eventually found her to be more concerned with her own needs.

> ... While Eman was there [at NESH] from day to day, it seemed that it was all about how she could get herself into the media such as Facebook, meetings and other public relations work. She was there day to day unless she rang in and said she was away somewhere such as Canberra meeting various Ministers or in New Zealand or Queensland doing some related work.[358]

The misuse by a public official of the NESH car by using it for personal use could constitute corrupt conduct. In his submissions, Counsel Assisting the Commission contended for a finding of corrupt conduct to be made against Richard Sharobeem in relation to his use of the NESH car. However, in determining whether such a finding should be considered, the Commission:

> ... took into account his youth at the time and the special nature of his relationship with his mother. He was only twenty three years old at the time of his employment at NESH, and twenty five years old at the time of giving evidence at the public inquiry. He is therefore a young man with his whole life ahead of him. The evidence showed that Ms Sharobeem was very closely involved in all aspects of his life. Not only did she organise his work for him, but she also controlled his finances to the extent that she kept his receipts for his purchases in her own handbag. In the Commission's view, it would be fair to say that she directed Richard Sharobeem's life to a great extent, and he essentially did what his mother told him to do. It is therefore quite possible that, had it not been for Ms Sharobeem's strong influence, he may well have acted differently in relation to his use of the NESH vehicle. Accordingly, in all the circumstances, the Commission

determined to exercise its discretion and did not make any corrupt conduct finding against Richard Sharobeem in relation to his use of the NESH vehicle.[359]

Two Zombie Boards, Two Broken Charities

Julie Watton was a NESH Board member. She was the first witness and gave evidence on 1 May 2017. It is clear she did not know what her board responsibilities were:

> **ICAC:** Did you ask to look at supporting documentation in relation to reimbursements?
> **WATTON:** No, but in hindsight with board training I would of.
> **ICAC:** Did anybody in, from the beginning of say 2015 when FACS raised concerns with NESH, did anyone on the board ask to look at invoices that had been submitted in support of reimbursement?
> **WATTON:** Not that I'm aware of.
> **ICAC:** Was the Board aware of the amount of equipment that was necessary to conduct the service?
> **WATTON:** I don't believe so.
> **ICAC:** Did the Board have any understanding of what was actually required to conduct the service, namely NESH first of all?
> **WATTON:** No. It doesn't look like it.[360]

The following day at the ICAC hearing, Delilah Paredo, another Board member, gave evidence of board stacking by Sharobeem:

> **ICAC:** When you started on the Board at Immigrant Women's Health Service ... did you talk to [Sharobeem] about what you would be doing on the Board?
> **PAREDO:** Not, not really.
> **ICAC:** Did she ask you to be a treasurer?
> **PAREDO:** Yeah, she say if you can be a treasurer, and I ask, I never be in, in, in that position anything, no, no need to doing anything, just sign the cheque when, when is required.
> **ICAC:** Was it the case that she only asked you to sign cheques?
> **PAREDO:** Yeah.
> **ICAC:** What else did she ask you to do while you were a Board member at IWHS?
> **PAREDO:** Nothing.[361]

Audrey Lai had worked for Centrelink and its predecessor organisations for thirty three years until her retirement. Active in local welfare issues, she chaired at times both the IWHS and the NESH Boards. Her evidence was significant to the issue of the absence of financial accountability.

Sharobeem's high media profile made Board members starry-eyed. Perhaps there was a little bit of fear there too:

AUDREY LAI (AL): Well, I must say that one thing that was lacking in our Board meetings was the financial reporting ... we would only mainly talk about the services ... so she would tell us what was happening and, and also all the extra meetings she was having, you know, with the Minister and things like that. She would also, like, tell us not to worry as Board members, that everything was going smoothly.
ICAC: And how often would she give you and the Board members those assurances about the service running well?
AL: When we had the, the two-monthly meetings. Like, I had no reason or none of us had any reason to, to doubt her because like, you see her high profile in the media before when she had, you know, appeared on the *60 Minutes* regarding to the child brides, child marriage issue, I mean she talked on SBS radio and television and like, you know, she had, she was on a domestic violence committee for the, the ah, Premier of New South Wales, so like we had no reason to doubt that everything was good and, you know, mmm.
ICAC: Did you trust her?
AL: I did, I did, yes.
ICAC: Did you know if the other Board members trusted her?
AL: I did, yeah.
ICAC: Did Ms Sharobeem at these Board meetings ever seek approval for expenses incurred by the organisation?
AL: Not really.
ICAC: Do you know if she sought approval for reimbursement to her account for expenses she had paid on her credit card, prior to being reimbursed?
AL: No, not prior to being reimbursed, no ... But she did provide us a big pile of invoices that we had to rubberstamp sign ... you know.
ICAC: Was there an incident where the bookkeeper had raised something with Ms Sharobeem and Ms Sharobeem had become

upset with her, that you're aware of?
AL: I think Neth [Chanthalangsy], the last bookkeeper ... did want to sign as the bookkeeper and when, when we asked her why she said you, you will find out when the auditor goes through the books. So I didn't know what to make of it at that time. [362]

The zombie boards at IWHS and NESH were waving through all Sharobeem's illegal purchases. They also allowed her to conduct her own "performance reviews". These amounted to the Board members listening rapturously to Sharobeem's glossed-up accounts of her celebrity moments when she met this politician or went on that media program.

ICAC: Did the Board ever conduct a formal review of Ms Sharobeem's day-to-day work at the IWHS?
AL: No ... we did do like, well, a performance like appraisal thing at the end of the year.
ICAC: And what did that involve?
AL: Very informal because, you know, she would say oh, she's doing all these wonderful things.
ICAC: It was all verbal was it, was any of it written down, the review?
AL: No.
ICAC: So a chat with her?
AL: Yeah ... she would say oh, yes, I'm doing all these wonderful things and, you know, and we had already seen some of her work in the media and ... from the Minister and the – even the Fairfield Mayor ... we did sort of say oh, you know, you should like, in hindsight we'll say do some selfcare because you're working too hard and take a holiday and things like that, you know.
ICAC: ... you didn't check on the way in which she was doing her job did you?
AL: Not day to day, no.

If either of the boards had summoned the courage to ask the hard questions, the answers would have shocked them. Their CEO was spending most of the program money and both charities were in freefall.

Audrey Lai's naïve complicity in Sharobeem's crimes also extended to the regular practice of signing stacks of blank cheques. Sharobeem used one of these cheques to buy the new

Honda City car for her son, Richard, for $18,000, which Lai did not know about or approve.[363]

The following email was sent in the dying days when the situation at both IWHS and NESH was terminal. The context is that Sharobeem bought a car with NESH funds for the sole use of her son. This caused an understandable grievance with other staff. The email shows that Lai stood behind Sharobeem long after the facts justified such misplaced loyalty:

> From: "Lai, Audrey"
> To: Nada Damcevska, Julie Watton, Nevine Ghaly, Houda Moukhaiber [NESH Board members], "Dr. Eman Sharobeem."
> Date: Wed, 19 Aug 2015
>
> Dear all,
> I finally got a chance to speak with Eman (we are both very busy) and was able to understand more about NESH cars. NESH always had 2 cars, when the Ford was updated to the Honda. Nevine [NESH project officer and whistleblower] did not want to drive the Honda and preferred to drive the Mazda and accordingly Eman asked a staff member [Richard Sharobeem] to drive the car and keep it on the road. I learnt from Nevine that Emannuel [NESH community worker] went to work appointment in Campbelltown by the train because Richard has the car, that is why I thought of the car pool. Nevine will set up the booking form for the car in the office.
> Nevine, I would suggest in the future that you discuss any issues like this with Eman directly as NESH advisor and CEO. With governance issues, you can speak with the Board, while with day to day running of the office issues, you can speak with Eman, with her vast experience, [she] is to remain the advisor on a day to day basis.
>
> Regards,
> Audrey Lai

The following exchange at the ICAC hearing with Julie Watton, the NESH Board member, shows the extraordinary procedure Sharobeem insisted upon for the signing off of her illicit expenditure.

WATTON: I remember we were in Eman's office, having some type of meeting. I don't know when it was, though. And there was a whole pile of paperwork that was on her desk that she asked if we would sign for her. But the payments had already been made so it was being approved after the payment had already been made.
ICAC: What did you think about that particular process?
WATTON: We brought it up and said that's not the way that things have to happen ... one person can't prepare and authorise the payments.
ICAC: How many invoices or documents do you say were on Ms Sharobeem's desk?
WATTON: There was quite a pile of them.
ICAC: How thick? ... So you're indicating about 10 centimetres?
WATTON: ... each of us were given a pile to sign.
ICAC: Did Ms Sharobeem tell you when those payments had been made?
WATTON: No.
ICAC: Did [Sharobeem] tell you what the invoices were for?
WATTON: I didn't look at all of them ... I [was] mainly aware of the one to do with the Westmead Hospital ...
ICAC: Were you told what the payment was for?
WATTON: It was supposed to be something for the – presenting a paper at Westmead Hospital [payment was for son Richard's liposuction].[364]

How long was this pillaging to last?

The Slow Downfall

Although justice did not knock sharply on Sharobeem's door until 2016, 2015 was the real year of her downfall. It came slowly and with great resistance particularly from members of the IWHS and NESH boards, who stayed in denial about Sharobeem's financial rapacity right to the very end. The respective NSW State Government departments, Health for IWHS and Family and Community Services (FACS) for NESH, took a lot of convincing that there was anything wrong and then when things became visibly bad, moved at turtle speed. Politicians continued to pop into the centres and get their photos and commendations in the local papers. This opportunistic behaviour continued to legitimise Sharobeem. Meanwhile she just kept on ripping public money out of the system for herself and her family.

The first signs that something was wrong occurred on 15 January 2015 with a visit to IWHS by Christine Pollachini, the Manager of Sydney South West Area Health Service, and her new boss, the ambitious and competent Josephine Chow. This was a meet and greet occasion as Chow had just assumed the position of Associate Director, Strategic Projects with IWHS's principal funder, the Health Department's South Western Sydney Local Health District (SWSLHD).[365] This meeting was a long time coming as Sharobeem kept putting it off. It was also a long time coming because SWSLHD had avoided site visits in favour of the lower level accountability test of accepting performance reports self-servingly generated by Sharobeem. These recorded preposterously high numbers of clients against all the categories, including groups, "drop-ins", telephone and face-to-face counselling. The Final ICAC Report found that the IWHS annual activity report for 2012–13 included: 18,500 clients attending groups, 8240 instances of telephone counselling, and 2,582 face-to-face counselling. ICAC commented:

> The last figure is noteworthy, given that Ms Sharobeem told the SWSLHD officers that she was the only IWHS employee at the Fairfield office who provided face-to-face counselling ... It is concerning that the SWSLHD apparently accepted these inflated figures for several years without question ...[366]

Chow gave evidence that she was surprised at the low numbers of clients and she asked Sharobeem for a weekly calendar of events.[367] Unbeknownst to the two officers they were witnessing a service in organisational decay. With a zombie board, a cowed staff and a CEO distracted by the glamour aspects of her job, what else could it be?

Chow and Pollachini returned at the end of January expecting to see more clients as school holidays had finished, but only saw "1 or 2".[368] By now both IWHS and NESH were hollowed out organisations just going through the motions. Their CEO was either on the celebrity circuit or counselling fee-paying clients who came to her in goodwill because they believed she was eminently qualified to help them. Chow and Pollachini missed all the red flags. All they appear to have done was to tell Sharobeem to stop reporting the English classes in the key performance indicators as they were not health related. For most of 2015, Sharobeem defaulted four times in meeting reporting deadlines back to SWSLHD.[369] SWSLHD did not allocate sufficient staff to oversee its funded organisations. At the time of the corrupt conduct, the SWSLHD funded twenty NGOs, yet only a 0.6 full-time equivalent position was responsible for overseeing these organisations.

The next month was business as usual for Sharobeem: an Australian Egyptian Council Forum, and a $3192 payment for cosmetics from The Lily Room.[370] But something unusual happened. Out of the blue, ICAC received an anonymous complaint which they relayed to FACS for investigation. Obviously unaware of the brewing storm, two days after ICAC received the complaint Sharobeem used public funds to pay $5948 to Westmead Hospital for her overweight son Richard's liposuction procedure. We will see that this bill played a big role in her downfall.

The local FACS office was also slowly emerging from bureaucratic hibernation. Libby Gallagher, from that office, wrote to the NESH Board and attached serious questions about governance and spending. FACS did not follow up on this. Gallagher went along to the IWHS Board meeting at the end of March. The Board was very solicitous of Sharobeem. They acknowledged her passion and worried about her overworking herself and asked her to take it easy. The letter of complaint from FACS about 2013 NESH budget issues was considered by the Board. Evidence was given at the ICAC hearing that Gallagher said that she didn't really look at anonymous complaints or letters. "They were not", she said "worth the paper they're written on".[371]

Sharobeem resigned suddenly from NESH soon after this meeting. NESH project officer, Nevine Ghaly said, "I remember an email sent from Eman Sharobeem to Audrey Lai (NESH Chair) and the Committee where she said she'd had enough of this and because of her health she couldn't go on with it etc., and needed Audrey to step up as the Chair".[372] This time, and for numerous occasions to follow, as justice moved closer, Sharobeem presented her Medicare card instead of her credit card.

In mid-April, the auditors, Boyd and Associates, wrote to the NESH Board advising them how they should be responding to the audit questions in the previously received FACS letter. At the same time, Sharobeem responded to her concerns about her so-called failing health by spending a massive $5000 of public money on cosmetics from The Lily Room.[373] IWHS, crumbling and disorganised, was visited by another politician looking for some reflected glory. This time it was the Hon. Sophie Cotsis from the NSW Legislative Council. Cotsis issued a completely misinformed statement in which she said:

> IWHS is at the forefront of addressing some of the most difficult issues confronting our society ... Dr Eman Sharobeem is a real-life super hero who has dedicated her life and considerable skill to helping some of the people most in need in our country.

Cotsis called on the NSW Minster for Multiculturalism, John Ajaka, to provide increased funding to IWHS and like organisations in the June 2015 budget.[374] One can only imagine what would have happened if IWHS and NESH, both in absolute moral and financial decline, found themselves suddenly awash with new government funding.

By now the picture was becoming clearer about Sharobeem's hold over the IWHS Board. At the meeting on 5 June, Audrey Lai, IWHS chair, and Sharobeem, announced to the credulous gathering that IWHS had won an award from NAPCAN, the National Association for the Prevention of Child Abuse and Neglect, for its multicultural parenting program. The problem was that this program never existed. After taking in this "wonderful news" the Board solicitously advised Sharobeem to take as long as she needed to recover from an operation she was to have at end of June.

Soon after this, in response to some awkward questions being asked by Christine Pollachini from SWSLHD, the regional Health Department office, Sharobeem directed Watfa El-Baf, the part-time administrator at IWHS, to alter the agency's client statistics so that they would appear to be doing more business than they were.[375] A week later Sharobeem issued the same instruction to the other administrator at IWHS, Marie Abboud.[376]

With her back to the wall, Sharobeem needed a scapegoat, and fast. She started to spin a story that the IWHS and NESH bookkeeper, Chanthaneth Chanthalangsy ("Neth"), was the person responsible for all of the centre's financial problems. It was a very stressful time for Neth. She started confiding in Nevine Ghaly, the NESH project officer, about dodgy claims Sharobeem was making. She particularly referred to the Westmead Hospital bill for Sharobeem's son's operation. The Board accepted Sharobeem's story and started to put further pressure on Neth who resigned soon after this.[377]

At the 2 September meeting the Board was still holding fast to its CEO. The minutes show that further concerns were expressed that she was working too hard. For the first time Sharobeem acknowledged that she had been using her personal credit card for work purposes as the IWHS credit card limit was too low. The Board's response? Sharobeem was told to stop doing that and the credit limit on the IWHS card was increased!

A week later, Nathan Boyd wrote to Sharobeem expressing his concern that there had been too many instances of incorrect transfer of funds between NESH and IWHS. He said, "As part of my audit, I will review in detail to ensure that expenses have been paid from the correct entity". His audit report that followed showed that many of the problems found in the 2014 audit were not addressed (particularly double payments and phantom facilitators).

With the ethical Neth out of the picture, the role of moral leadership fell to the part-time administrators, Ms El-Baf and Ms Abboud. They prepared a complaint to Pollachini. Now in damage control, Sharobeem paid back $31,940 in three separate payments shortly after the complaint went to Pollachini.[378] These refunds were not driven by a sense of remorse. She was not a changed woman. On 6 October, she emailed Ms El-Baf, directing her to add 20 more people to each of the groups that were supposed to be running at IWHS.[379] The next day Ms El-Baf asked for the names of these phantom attendees but got no reply from Sharobeem.

Just after Sharobeem refunded a further $9,738, the IWHS Board held an urgent meeting to talk about the auditor's grim findings. The minutes are revealing. The Board was not going to throw their star player off the field that easily.

1. Noted that Eman has admitted that she went under name EMMA ADLY as people find it hard to pronounce "Eman".
2. Board resolves to ask auditor whether it is OK for someone to work under more than one name.
3. Eman to return all monies paid to Emma Adly.

4. In future Eman to only use her known name.

By taking this extraordinary tack the individual Board members exposed themselves to the charge of criminal conspiracy.

Firing Sharobeem bullets, the Board then targeted Neth, the previous bookkeeper:

5. Why did bookkeeper pay duplicate reimbursements?
6. Why did bookkeeper pay without supporting evidence?
7. Board to ask Eman to repay duplicate reimbursements.
8. Board noted that Eman has repaid $18,000 for car from Peter Warren.
9. Board proposes to appoint office manager.

The Board again had exposed itself to legal action for concealing a crime.

At the next IWHS meeting on 4 November, with Sharobeem present, the Board acknowledged the tireless advocacy work of Sharobeem for CALD (culturally and linguistically diverse) women. Incredibly they were still singing from their culpable CEO's songbook:

1. That she has been too busy to check payments.
2. That bookkeeper is taking bills from her desk and paying them into her account!
3. Bookkeeper not able to code reimbursements correctly.
4. Staff are getting into her office and paying the bills.
5. Eman says that she is now methodically checking all payment requests, monitoring her account and has employed a new bookkeeper who is great!
6. Board again acknowledged that Eman's workload means the financials are not being adequately controlled. Resolves to appoint office manager.
7. Eman has drafted a new policy guideline that addresses all the auditor's concerns.
8. Board acknowledged that financial control has improved and there are now better communications.

By now Nathan Boyd knew that there was something seriously wrong. He also knew that the IWHS zombie Board would continue to cover for Sharobeem. On the same day as the 4 November board meeting, and unbeknownst to the Board, he contacted the SWSLHD's chief financial officer. The funding agency finally moved quickly. The CFO reported Boyd's concerns to the NSW Police and, on 6 November 2015, SWSLHD quarantined all funds to IWHS.

Despite this stubborn loyalty from the Board, things from this point onwards started to unravel quickly. A week after the last board meeting, Sharobeem convened her last showcase symposium. It was called the "The Paradigm Shift of Family Violence within CALD Communities". Speakers included Marise Payne, then Minister for Defence and Pru Goward, then NSW Minister for Women.

The next day, Nathan Boyd presented his second auditor report for 2014–15, listing many spending concerns:

> We have issued a *qualified auditor's opinion*. We were unable to obtain sufficient appropriate audit evidence regarding a significant amount of expenses. As a result, we are unable to provide an opinion on a number of items presented on the Assets and Liabilities statement.[380]

In response, the Board called in forensic accountants Furzer and Crestani. Sharobeem declined a request to attend a Board meeting to discuss payment irregularities discovered by Boyd, citing illness.[381] She also declined a request to be interviewed by Mr. Katehos, the forensic accountant, citing illness.

The IWHS and NESH ships were sinking. In December, Richard, her son, resigned from IWHS, soon followed by the Chair, Audrey Lai, who resigned from both the IWHS Board and the NESH Board. Finally, Sharobeem resigned in February 2016.

It was this month that ICAC took over the investigation into allegations of Sharobeem's corruption. On 16 February they took their first of thirty five statements. This one was from Nada Damcevska-Stamenkovska, a social worker, who at different times was on the Boards of NESH and IWHS. A month later FACS terminated its funding agreement with NESH.[382]

In March, the Furzer and Crestani forensic audit recommended that since the misspending was so serious, the Board had only two options: ask Sharobeem to resign or dismiss her and refer the matter to NSW Police. The Board decided to ask for her resignation, "as she had repaid $62,000".[383] Even with the end in sight Sharobeem still continued a public life, particularly representing Multicultural NSW at various ethnic gatherings: Australian Bhutanese Conference, Rath Yatra Festival of Chariots, the Islamic High Council of Australia and The Islamic Charity Project Association, to name a few. She was even appointed by SBS as their Community Engagement Manager. Two weeks before IWHS closed its doors for the last time Sharobeem cut an interview with SBS Amharic. She was the model of coolness and eloquence on the show as she recycled her rags to riches story.

On 17 August, ICAC executed a search warrant on her home and found numerous goods purchased on the IWHS credit cards. In September, she sold 92 Smart Street Fairfield, the headquarters of IWHS that she had bought secretly for $660,000. The sale price was $1.3million.

Two days after the sale of 92 Smart Street Fairfield, Sharobeem was on the Channel 10 program, *The Project*. It was another case of lazy journalism meets clever, articulate fabricator. The panel sat back and allowed Sharobeem to retell her fictionalised biography, which by now was her *motif*. She shared her bogus experiences as a former child bride and said: "After all these years I'm still carrying the residue of pain inside me". She talked about following "God's way". She carried off this pretence with such convincing composure, just two weeks after ICAC raided her house and found all the stolen goods.

In November, she resigned from the Community Relations Commission and Multicultural NSW, citing personal and health reasons. On 21 November, she was made to attend a compulsory examination before ICAC. With this brooding nemesis circling, she moved fast to hide her ill-gotten wealth. She transferred $499,000 into her son Charlie's account. He then forwarded $529,485 to the wife of Eman's nephew, Dalia Saeed Kamel, in Nasr City Egypt. The authorities were not quick enough to grab this money before it went offshore but in mid-February 2017, NSW Supreme Court judge, Mr. Justice Davies issued orders to freeze all of Sharobeem's other assets pursuant to the NSW *Criminal Assets Recovery Act* 1990.[384]

Lies and Moral Indignation: Weapons of Choice for the Trapped

Sixteen months after her resignation Sharobeem was before what I regard as one of the most powerful and credible anti-corruption agencies in the world, the New South Wales Independent Commission against Corruption (ICAC). They established a formal inquiry, *Operation Tarlo*, to investigate corruption allegations against her when she was the CEO of IWHS and the Non-English-Speaking Housing Women's Scheme Inc (NESH).[385] *Operation Tarlo* hearings started on 1 May 2017 before Acting Commissioner Reginald Blanch QC. The hearings finished in October 2017 with final submissions.[386] The damning final report was tabled by ICAC in the NSW Parliament on 19 September 2018.

When Amanda Kate Smith was confronted with her charity fraud she confessed immediately and cooperated with the police and courts. Eman Sharobeem posed a more difficult challenge for ICAC because in pre-hearing testimony, and on the stand, she repeatedly lied and expressed, in the strongest possible terms, her moral indignation at the allegations she was faced with. So common was the lying, and so strong the moral indignation that if her defence team were to have made a submission that Sharobeem was suffering from a psychiatric condition known as confabulation, they may well have got a hearing from the ICAC Commissioner on that point.[387]

The following format, relying on extracts from transcripts of the ICAC hearing, puts the reader back into the ICAC hearing room:

Questioned about falsifying service statistics.[388]

> **ICAC:** You intentionally inflated the figures for New South Wales Health didn't you?
> **Eman Sharobeem (ES):** Absolutely never ... no, no, no, no ... See you can try to tarnish my reputation. You can try to accuse me, abuse me, bully me, harass me, terrorise me but you cannot take away the fact that in my life I only raised two sons and worked for women migrants and refugees and helped and saved many, many life (*sic*). You cannot take this away from me until the grave. You cannot, and you will not do that.

ICAC: You intentionally falsified figures to the Department of Health.
ES: [I] ... disagree with you. My work is known. My work is shown. The lives I've saved. People can come from different directions and they come now to say how much I did and put my life out there and, and sacrificed a lot, a lot of my youth and years to save women and girls. Do not come now, sir, and try to take that away from me. You have no right. You have no right.
ICAC: You intentionally falsified the figures to raise your own profile, didn't you?
ES: Never ... I did not want to raise my own profile. I was pushed to come out and talk about my childhood and what happened to me as a victim of, of forced marriage, as a victim of, of, of female genital mutilation, as a victim to come out and help Australian women and girls and I did and I cannot regret that because many lives were saved. Do not take that away from me.[389]

Questioned about her Classic Holiday membership.

ICAC: Do you understand that I'm going to ask you some questions about your Classic Club Holiday membership?
ES: Please ask me.
ICAC: You said that you purchased the holiday membership for the organisation [IWHS].
ES: Yes.
ICAC: ... Are you now suggesting that no one travelled on the Classic Club membership from the Immigrant Women's Health Service?
ES: ... when I bought [Classic Club membership] it was ... to giving women something at the end of the year and that's what we tried to do as health information service, but at the same time circumstances didn't allow this to happen. That's what I remember.
ICAC: What circumstances did not allow it to happen.
ES: I can't remember why it didn't happen.
ICAC: What are you talking about, what circumstances are you talking about, Ms Sharobeem?
ES: ... I'm trying to make sense but ...
ICAC: Well, try a little harder.
ES: I can't remember.
ICAC: ... Ms Sharobeem, that's because what you're suggesting to

this Commission about purchasing the membership for members of Immigrant Women's Health Service is a lie isn't it?

ES: No.

ICAC: Ms Sharobeem, did you purchase the membership for yourself and family?

ES: ... I would like to remind you, sir, that I was the only full-time worker doing all and everything in an organisation, including speaking up against all the form of violation against women.

ICAC: That's got nothing to do with the question I'm asking you.

ES: It got, it got a lot to do ... with the size of things required from me as a human being. Please remember that you are working certain hours and getting certain pay. I, I was underpaid and overworked. So if any wrongdoing happened, including not offering or not proceeding, it's not because it's my intention. It's because I was overstretched. And I was also doing a lot of volunteer work. It's, I don't want you to feel that I did this deliberately.

ICAC: Are you suggesting that because you were overworked that those were the circumstances that led to this service, the membership, not being extended to the IWHS clients?

ES: ... Many, many of the mistakes because I was overstretched.

ICAC: So because you were overworked, you're saying that you then used the membership for your personal benefit, are you?

ES: No, no. The membership was there and as a worker of the organisation I can use it as well. I am also a client of the organisation in some other events.

ICAC: No, you are not, Ms Sharobeem ... You are the chief executive officer ... of the Immigrant Women's Health Service, do you agree with that?

ES: No, I don't.

ICAC: You don't agree?

ES: I don't. I have to set the record straight right now, sir. Every time I am called a CEO of the organisation, this is actually wrong. I might have the title of a CEO but I never had any benefit as a CEO. The CEO as a title was given to me just because of the number of things and the number of position I was elevated to, just as a prestige. But I was never, ever being treated as one. So every time I am in the media or here (not transcribable) CEO, this is a big title and big responsibility. I was doing everything and anything in the organisation. I wasn't paid as a CEO. I didn't have entitled as a

CEO. It was something because of the threaten we were receiving from the Health Department and other funding body that the funding is going to be cut to small organisation. The organisation was trying to elevate its position so that we have that.[390]

Questioned about Eternity Jewellers.

ICAC: The Commission has evidence that between 22 May 2014 and 18 February 2015 receipts totalling $29,695 from Eternity Jewellers were submitted in support of reimbursements to your account. I took you to this invoice on the last occasion and we step by step went through each particular day and proved that you had used IWHS funds to pay for this particular, what is it, a diamond necklace for $20,000? It cost $20,000 didn't it so, what were you on, $80,000 about weren't you?
ES: I'm glad you said it out loud to the world to hear that I was on ... The point is also that in this year I was after 20 years of being a single woman finally married and I was able to afford this with the support of my husband. That's why together we bought these items from Eternity because that was my first diamond purchase he's giving me ...
THE COMMISSIONER: I think the proposition that's being put to you is asking you to explain how when you're on a small salary you embark on a, and even allowing for the fact that you're now married, you're not a person who is awash with money, if we can put it that way ... And yet you have spent about 30,000, 30-something thousand dollars on jewellery and none of that has come out of your bank account from 2014 until the audit was done and you repaid it some couple of years later. How could you not be aware is the question of the fact that you hadn't actually had to pay for such large objects?
ES: ... the truth of the matter is in [our Coptic Egyptian] culture the husband have (*sic*) to buy gifts and buy – participate in the furniture and the making of the home. Because it was my home and it was settled and I had the children living with us, when he married me he only bought me the ring and then he participated in this purchase so as a man of the house he would be coming with jewellery and gifts to his wife equally to her value as we say in our culture. That is the truth of the matter because he didn't buy anything else in the house. He came in and it was everything set for him. That's all the cultural perspective part.

But the other thing is during that time, sir, especially in this year, my psychological and physical wellbeing was very deteriorated and it's a well-known fact. Everybody in the area knew that. I even in pictures appear very deteriorated in many of the pictures. So basically I wasn't really following up everything and anything, and I already declared to you, sir, before that I was (not transcribable). In a matter of fact, the cash in my hand was always given to me by my husband, and the house and everything else was managed by my son and my husband. So I wasn't really looking closely into this two years into what's happening or what's going on. I was very tired and deteriorated, hence the operation I had in 2015 and being very ill before that. So that's the actual reason. But with Eternity I just (not transcribable) that it's my purchase. My husband supported that.

... the frank point is the Eternity, it was my husband trying to gift me back because he didn't participate in anything in the house, and buying me diamond is culturally appropriate in our culture.

THE COMMISSIONER: But you're the one who bought it, weren't you?

ES: Yeah, because it's my choice and then he would pay me cash, and usually he always gives me cash. Always. And that's why I always had money in my hand. But I am not rich and I have zero dollar in the bank now and (not transcribable).[391]

Questioned about Eye Concepts.

ICAC: In relation to Eye Concepts, can I ask you first, was that where you went for your personal optometry?

ES: Yes.

ICAC ... do you understand that $2,196 worth of receipts were submitted in support of reimbursements to your account for the IWHS account?

ES: It wasn't submitted.

ICAC: Over four years you didn't realise that you had submitted receipts from your personal optometrist?

ES: Over 12 years this organisation was Eman Sharobeem to the extent that people came to me and said the organisation will close if you would leave. I was the only one doing everything from A to Z, that's what I understand.[392]

Questioned about her honesty.

THE COMMISSIONER: Are you a dishonest person?
ES: Absolutely not. Never. I am known to be honest and credible to a lot of people, thousands of people. I wouldn't, sir, for $1,000, for 1,000 or 400 or $42 jeopardise my reputation. I wouldn't. For the money of the world, I wouldn't.
THE COMMISSIONER: So what's being suggested here is that you have been basically plundering the resources of the [Immigrant] Women's Service for your own benefit and that of your family and that's why it's been worthwhile for you to do it?
ES: No, sir, I didn't do that. For many years since I started in this organisation the organisation had become the place where I invest all my time. I didn't have a husband, all my life was work as a husband and people said Eman is married to her work and her children and I spent most of my time over there, day and night, working. People know if I'm not in the office I'm outside advocating for women and girls. That's why when anyone talks about abusing women I feel like this is the actual crime they are putting on my shoulder. I didn't.
THE COMMISSIONER: Well, that is being suggested, that you have in fact deprived these women of the assistance that they otherwise would have obtained by using the money that you have taken that you shouldn't have taken. That's the matter that's being looked at?
ES: And it didn't happen, sir, it didn't happen.[393]

Questioned about the quantum of the fraud.

ICAC: Between 2008 and 2016, the total of reimbursements, facilitator fees, including your sons' facilitator fees for Richard and Charlie, and your salary, the amount you obtained from the IWHS has been totalled by the Commission. It comes to $1,196,781.81. That's a lot of money, isn't it?
ES: I can't accept this figure ... Please stop trying to frame me. I know that you're doing your job but please do not put in the public figure, public mind those figures because it's not true. It's a lie. When you calculate how much we received, when we calculate how much I delivered to the organisation, it doesn't weigh back. I delivered way more than four, five, six million dollars to the organisation because of my work.[394]

Questioned about her false qualifications.

ICAC: Can I show you your CV ...
ES: Sure, yes. Sure.
ICAC: Do you agree that the reference to you having completed a thesis in psychology is wrong?
ES: Yes, it's wrong.
ICAC: Do you agree that you having studied a Minor in Community Management at the American University in Cairo is wrong?
ES: Yes, it's a mistake, of course.
ICAC: Do you agree that the Master in Community Management at the American University is wrong?
ES: Yes, it is a mistake indeed.
ICAC: You never completed your degree at the University of Technology did you in 1994?
ES: No, I didn't.
ICAC: So that is wrong isn't it?
ES: It's a mistake, yes, I agree.
ICAC: ... And do you accept that you've sent the email knowing that it had contained a false attachment?
ES: It appeared this way, yes ... I am in full agreement that what you're saying is right but at the same time who would do such a mistake.
ICAC: I suggest to you that you did this intentionally, Ms Sharobeem.
ES: What did I gain from it? Nothing.[395]

Questioned about her cutting receipts.

As noted above, Sharobeem was in the practice of cutting the details of what she bought from her receipts for personal shopping and then leaving these cut receipts for a staff member to reimburse her. This way hundreds of thousands of dollars found their way into Sharobeem's personal banking account. On 10 May 2017, the following exchange took place at the ICAC hearing:

THE COMMISSIONER: Okay. Now, you want to say, do you, that the receipts that you put out were full receipts and somebody else cut them?
ES: Absolutely. I left everything on the desk.
ICAC: And the effect of them cutting them was to ... delete the

information that would tell anybody else whether it was private or not, and you got the benefit of it?
ES: I didn't get the benefit of it. I wish I did. I wish, I wish I did, my own mind
ICAC: Well, you got the benefit of the money that was refunded.
ES: Which is mistakenly refunded by me. And as soon as I was told about any mistaken refund, it was reimbursed directly and I have evidence. Sir, also ...
ICAC: Just, just a moment ...
ES: ... if I want to do that ...
ICAC: ... Just a moment. Just a moment. This is what we're looking at ... $2,800.
ES: Yes, it's a lot ...
ICAC: It's a huge amount. It's a lot of money ...
ES: I'm sorry, I'm just under the shock, just shock of knowing that and (not transcribable)
ICAC: Well, there may be more shocks coming. So just calm down.
ES: Oh, dear ...
ICAC: I'm still in June 2014. I'll show you some transfers on page 322. And, Ms Sharobeem, you need to appreciate that I'm showing you transfers of money that went into your personal account in one month?
ES: Am I stupid person to do such a mistake to pay for ...
THE COMMISSIONER: Just wait for the question?
ES: ... I'm sorry, I'm sorry, I'm just overwhelmed. I can't believe what happened to me and why I'm framed like that. ... This is too much ...
THE COMMISSIONER: We'll adjourn for five minutes.[396]

Questioned as to why she used different names.

THE COMMISSIONER: Can I just ask you why these reimbursements are in the name of Emma Adly?
ES: I um, sign on the invoices on the time sheet for the facilitator, the amount is going to my bank account and I put the different name so I wouldn't create a storm with the staff that I work as a facilitator as well, just to, just I, maybe it was my way to avoid being questioned by the staff that you work extra or why aren't we working extra like you, because they didn't have the skills to deliver what I was delivering ...[397]

Added to the implausibility of this response is the fact that Sharobeem had no training nor experience in facilitation herself.

She treated herself well, but not her staff, two of whom approached her on numerous times to make them permanent/ part-time employees. In evidence, Watfa El-Bal, employed at IWHS as an administrator, September 2005 to June 2016, said:

> Eman would refuse by explaining that the Management Committee would not accept that, and by saying: "God knows how I struggle to keep this organisation on its feet. The organisation doesn't have money and the grants given to IWHS were too little". Marie [Abboud, IWHS administrator 2001–2016] and I never have had any entitlements for 7 years, such as superannuation, sick days, holidays ... Until Eman's resignation in 2016, our hourly rate was $20.[398]

Questioned about the illegal payments to her and her sons.

> **ICAC:** ... I was asking you questions about facilitator payments, and do you recall that I said to you in summary that about a hundred thousand had been claimed by you over June 2014 and March 2015? Do you remember that?
> **ES:** I remember what you said ... I paid it back.
> **ICAC:** Ms Sharobeem, you agreed in your compulsory examination and I think in May this year that the facilitator or the alias for the facilitator Rachie Kakel was your son Richard. Correct?
> **ES:** I explained that.
> **ICAC:** Was Charl Gamal your son Charlie Sharobeem?
> **ES:** I said that to the Commission last time.
> **ICAC:** Was Rachie Kakel your son Richard Sharobeem?
> **ES:** I said that to the Commission but the auditor had no right to ask me if I have any relation with anyone.
> **ICAC:** You knew that they were both receiving payments for facilitator work didn't you?
> **ES:** How would I know? I organised the payment for them.
> **ICAC:** And you didn't tell the auditor who they really were because those payments were dishonest weren't they?
> **ES:** No, that's not true. The auditor didn't even ask me.
> **ICAC:** Why did you use the name Emy Adel to claim your facilitator fees then?
> **ES:** I explained that before.

ICAC: Well, why did you do it?
ES: I explained that before.
ICAC: Explain it to me again.
ES: I explained before to the Commission.
ICAC: What's the explanation? What is the explanation for it?
ES: Can I ask just to satisfy my limited ability, if I answer the question to the Commission why I'm asked again. What's that, to satisfy who and why except to keep abusing me and interrogating me and, and inhumanely to a great extent. Why?
THE COMMISSIONER: If it's a simple answer that you've given before just repeat the answer that you gave before.
ES: This Commission is against all forms of human rights, isn't it? This is just to abuse people (not transcribable), isn't it?
THE COMMISSIONER: Just calm down. Just stay calm for a moment. Would you like a glass of water?
ICAC: Between May of 2014 and March of 2015, you had transferred to your account $99,685 in relation to facilitator fees for Emy Adel, Eman West and Emma Adly. What do you say about that?
ES: I did the work. I delivered the service. Women and family were served and received full service from me. I got paid. This is not the period I delivered the service only, but I did not claim any things before and that's why it was crammed in this year, as it was indicated before. The auditor indicated that he doesn't accept this, and during my illness he bullied me to pay back and I did pay it back
ICAC: Ms Sharobeem, moving on to your sons, between April 2011 and March of 2015, in relation to your son, Richard Sharobeem, $34,050 was claimed for facilitator fees. What's your response to that?
ES: My son delivered the service, delivered the service to the organisation, he did what was intended from him to do and deliver what was requested from him, whatever the task that was requested, and he received the money.
ICAC: Ms Sharobeem, from November of 2009 to February of 2015 your son, Charlie Sharobeem, was transferred $7,750 in relation to facilitator fees. What do you say about that?
ES: My son delivered the service, the service was requested from him was fully obtained by the service, Immigrant Women's Health, and he received his fees.

ICAC: What do you say about your son's evidence at the compulsory examination, that is, Charlie Sharobeem, he said that he never worked at the IWHS. Your son said that, you're saying that he did work?
ES: He said he didn't work as a facilitator and I, as I explained before, the word facilitator is the term we use for bookkeeping purposes only. It doesn't mean that all our contractors would know that the word facilitator is used for our bookkeeping.[399]

This congestion of moral indignation and lies had no impact on the eventual ICAC findings.

Eman Sharobeem's Date with Justice

The *Operation Tarlo* report was tabled in the NSW Parliament on 19 September 2018.[400] It was damning of Sharobeem's conduct, finding twenty-four instances of serious corruption:

1. Between 2009 and 2015, improperly exercising her official functions to benefit herself by arranging to obtain up to $443,000, through transfers to her bank account, from IWHS by way of reimbursement for the cost of goods and services she had purchased for personal use, knowing that she was not entitled to such reimbursements.
2. Between February and June 2015, improperly exercising her official functions to benefit herself by arranging for the transfer of funds totalling $13,500 from IWHS to Andrew's Designer Jewellery, knowing that the payments related to the purchase of jewellery for personal use and that she was not entitled to use IWHS funds for that purpose.
3. Between 2010 and 2014, improperly exercising her official functions to benefit herself by arranging for the transfer of funds totalling $3,850 from IWHS to a wardrobe supplier, knowing that the payments related to the purchase of wardrobes for personal use and that she was not entitled to use IWHS funds for that purpose.
4. In about December 2013, improperly exercising her official functions by submitting an invoice for $210 to IWHS, which she knew to be false, in order to obtain payment from IWHS of $210 for pest control services at her home, knowing that she was not entitled to use IWHS funds for such a purpose.

5. In about June 2015, improperly exercising her official functions by submitting an invoice for $3,878 to IWHS, which she knew to be false, in order to obtain payment of $3,878 from IWHS for the purchase of a gate at her home, knowing that she was not entitled to use IWHS funds for such a purpose.
6. In March 2014, improperly exercising her official functions by submitting a receipt for $489 to IWHS, which she knew to be false, in order to obtain payment of $489 from IWHS to reimburse her for payment for a Classic Holiday Club VIP membership pass for herself, knowing that she was not entitled to use IWHS funds for such a purpose.
7. In June 2015, improperly exercising her official functions by submitting an invoice for $6,900 to IWHS, which she knew to be false, in order to obtain reimbursement of her personal credit card expense of $5,900, and to cover the use of the IWHS credit card to pay $1,000, for the purchase of a massage chair for her personal use, knowing that she was not entitled to use IWHS funds for such a purpose.
8. Between January 2009 and February 2016, improperly exercising her official functions to benefit herself or members of her family by using the IWHS credit card to pay $35,211.39 for personal goods and services, knowing that she was not entitled to use IWHS funds for such a purpose.
9. Between 2007 and 2016, improperly exercising her official functions to benefit herself or members of her family by causing payments totalling $31,157.87 to be made to Sydney Water Corporation and the State Debt Recovery Office (SDRO) by direct transfer of IWHS funds for personal expenses, knowing that she was not entitled to use IWHS funds for such a purpose.
10. Between May 2014 and March 2015, improperly exercising her official functions to obtain $99,685 through submitting invoices to IWHS, falsely claiming she had worked as a facilitator and causing payment of those invoices to be made to her by IWHS.
11. Between May 2014 and March 2015, improperly exercising her official functions to obtain $34,050 for her son, Richard Sharobeem, through submitting invoices to IWHS, falsely claiming he had worked as a facilitator and causing payment of those invoices to be made to him by IWHS.
12. Between May 2014 and February 2015, improperly exercising her official functions to obtain $7,750 for her son, Charlie Sharobeem,

through submitting invoices to IWHS, falsely claiming he had worked as a facilitator and causing payment of those invoices to be made to him by IWHS.

13. Between 2011 and 2015, improperly exercising her official functions to benefit herself by arranging for IWHS to pay $59,558.70 for work on her property at 92 Smart Street, Fairfield, knowing that, as owner of that property, those costs were her responsibility.
14. In 2014, improperly exercising her official functions to benefit herself by falsely stating in an application to the NSW Community Building Partnership that IWHS was the owner of her property at 92 Smart Street, Fairfield, with the intention of obtaining public funds to pay for work on her property.
15. In 2015, improperly exercising her official functions by knowingly falsifying statistics relating to the numbers of attendees for IWHS programs reported in the IWHS 2014–15 annual report, which she submitted to the South Western Sydney Local Health District (SWSLHD), knowing the false statistics would be relied on by NSW Health and the SWSLHD in determining IWHS's funding.
16. Between 2013 and 2015, improperly exercising her official functions by providing false statistics to the Smith Family in order to falsely represent to the Smith Family that IWHS had conducted the Multicultural Parenting Project and the Steps to Employment Project programs in accordance with its contractual obligations to the Smith Family.
17. Between January and April 2014, improperly exercising her official functions to transfer a total of $13,500 from the IWHS bank account into her bank account and then arranging for NESH to reimburse IWHS for that amount.
18. On 16 March 2015, improperly exercising her official functions to transfer $3,000 from the NESH bank account to her own bank account in order to reimburse herself for the $3,000 payment she made to Westmead Private Hospital for her son's medical procedure.
19. In late December 2014, improperly exercising her official functions to apply $18,000 in IWHS funds towards the purchase of a Mercedes car for her husband, Haiman Hammo, and then arranging for NESH to reimburse IWHS for that amount.
20. In early 2015, improperly exercising her official functions to arrange for her son, Richard Sharobeem, to be hired as a paid employee of NESH.

21. For a period of about six months from late December 2014 or early January 2015, improperly exercising her official functions to facilitate the exclusive use, including personal use, of a NESH motor vehicle by her son, Richard Sharobeem.
22. Between at least 2006 and 2016, improperly exercising her official functions by falsely representing herself to be a qualified psychologist with a PhD in psychology and providing psychological treatment to IWHS clients and patients referred to her.
23. In March 2011, knowingly submitting false academic qualifications to the CRC for the purpose of obtaining financial advantage by being appointed to the paid position of part-time commissioner of the CRC.
24. In about December 2012, knowingly submitting false academic qualifications to the ADB for the purpose of obtaining financial advantage by being appointed to the paid position of a board member of the ADB.[401]

Summarising these findings, the ICAC report said:

> The evidence establishes that Ms Sharobeem engaged in the above conduct wilfully and deliberately as a public official in the course of and in connection with her public office as the service manager or CEO of IWHS. She had no reasonable excuse or justification for her actions, which improperly conferred substantial personal benefits on herself and her family members. The nature of her misconduct was serious and warrants criminal sanction. This is because at the relevant time she was the head of an agency predominantly funded by public monies to provide important services to women and children in need, whose funds she deprived in large amounts motivated by greed to benefit herself and her family. The conduct was premeditated, systematic and continued over a substantial period of time.[402]

At the time of writing, ICAC has recommended that the NSW Director of Public Prosecutions take action against Sharobeem for the criminal offences of misconduct in public office, fraud, obtaining money by deception and giving false testimony.

Hindsight

Our journey into the land of giving is now at an end. Along with the holiday snaps from each chapter, the take home conclusion for the perceptive traveller is that there is deep trouble in this land. There is a smell about this land. On one mapping it is home to appalling social conditions such as poverty, violence, mental illness and homelessness whose existence, indeed persistent existence, brings shame to us all. On another mapping it is a land populated by Australians of goodwill, good Samaritans all, who work tirelessly to help their fellow men and women in trouble. Then there are the greedy carpetbaggers, business people fully briefed about our tax concession laws, looking to make a buck out of vulnerability (think the Bupa Group vignetted above). Also staking their claims in this troubled land are the fraudsters, as depicted in the case studies, who, answering the base siren calls of capitalism, steal charitable funds for private lifestyle purchases. The land also hosts very powerful anti-charity enclaves that rant, red-faced, about too many public funds going to the poor and otherwise disadvantaged (think Institute of Public Affairs). Then there are the big private corporations who set up non-transparent charitable trusts to direct our attention away from their ethically questionable core activities. The tie-in between Crown Casinos and the Packer Family Trust is a case in point. High up, away from the grim street level realities of violence, poverty and the like, in their plush CBD offices, are the ASX law firms and price-gouging ASX listed financial services companies, who act as money managers to some of Australia's largest charities. For example, the $17.5 million Danks Trust, established by Sir Aaron Danks in 1928 to fund poverty relief and education, says that its listed trustee company demanded a $160,000 annual fee, up from $29,000.[403] Finally, there is the charity regulator, the Australian Charities and Not-for-profits Commission, which has restricted jurisdiction across the whole of this land. The ACNC looks like a timid little boy looking up at an adult. Small, powerless, clueless and confused.

This land of giving is also a foggy and unreconnoitred land. It's hard to get around and it's hard to identify all the inhabitants. Charity is yet to become a serious research topic. We don't have in Australia the equivalent of the UK Charity Research Support Fund, which in 2018–19 will provide substantial government funding to universities who carry out research with charity partners.[404] We just seem to get along with flippant visualisations of charity being a land of good people helping out those not as fortunate. This book is intended to correct this serious knowledge gap by mounting a research expedition into the land of giving. If charity were like a jigsaw, any analysis of it would be straightforward. It is clearly not, so any investigation must measure up and treat charity with the complexity it deserves.

One way of doing this is to think about charity and also to think beyond charity. To place charity in crucial contexts, in other words, and to see how these contexts infuse meaning and shape the socio-political and economic dimensions of the land of giving. The way this was done in the book was to offer a triangulated analysis of the relationships between "charity", "fraud" and the "state". This book takes a particular route knowing that there are other routes that could be travelled and will indeed be travelled in the future.

Because there was only a very limited research precedent to follow, the book first paid special attention to the historical formation of charity as it appears today. It is a charity that has been shaped and reshaped in a crucible fired by the twin heat of a worldview comfortable with high government welfare intervention, where charity is a minor partner, and a counterview, one currently dominant, of small government welfare intervention, where the presence of gap-filling charities is now absolutely essential.

The retraction of government welfare services has had a profound and probably irreversible impact on the land of giving. Business, big charities and a swarm of mosquito size charities have colonised the vacant spaces left by a retreating social policy. This business-government partnership was depicted in the book as a fundamentally flawed paradigm. Recurrent or core funding first started to disappear from government welfare agencies in the 1980s. Then it started to disappear from the welfare charity sector. Enter the new model, *market welfare*. Funding that survived harsh and regular cutbacks reappeared in purchaser-provider contracts in which charities delivered specific outcomes tied to erratic government policy. This market model of charity suited business but NGO charities found it difficult, and they still do. Soon, the commercial providers began to be favoured and did not mind the gag clauses in the contracts.

Once inside this land of market welfare the task was to scan and record its size, shape and purpose. This was always going to be a challenge. Chapter Two presented the research difficulties here. First the current, legislative-based, definition of "charitable purpose" is so wide as to be unserviceable. About half of all registered charities don't do any charity as we understand the word. Chapter Two showed that about 32% of all registered charities have as their sole or main purpose the advancement of a religion. Similarly, about 20% of registered charities have education as their sole or main purpose. A comparison between Australia's largest "charity", the University of Melbourne, with current revenue around $2.3 billion, to Australia's smallest charity, the unheard-of Building Angels Ltd, with a revenue in 2016 of $10, makes no sense at all.

When we filter out non-charitable charities, such as the University of Melbourne, can we get closer to the question: what do *real* charities do? Unfortunately, no. Research that was referenced above, discovered that 46,716 registered charities presently claim that combatting homelessness is one of their core missions.[405] Eighty one percent of all charities registered with the national regulator say they are working in the homeless area! That simply does not stack up. There is a serious problem here.

If we do not know what charities do, as opposed to what they say they do, then detecting charity fraud is made that much harder. Chapter Three set the scene for the case studies by acknowledging that charity fraud is a special kind of fraud. It sits away from stealing from a business. It sits away from pension and benefit fraud, and it is certainly different from credit card and insurance claim fraud. For the charity fraudster to be effective, there must exist a clear and criminal intention to exploit the good intentions of the donor and thereby display a sociopathic indifference to the needy who won't get the charitable services because the money to fund them was stolen by the fraudsters to buy fridges and Mercedes cars. This makes charity fraud that much more insidious. Its psychological consequences can be far-reaching. The donor stung in a charity fraud may abandon further acts of charity and may even embrace a future negative view of human nature.

By referencing research and scanning various databases, a very general profile of charity fraud was able to be presented. We simply don't know the amount of money and material resources intercepted on its way to recipients by charity fraudsters in Australia. The Scamwatch figure for 2018 was over $200,000. But this is a low reliability figure and the tip of the iceberg because it relies on motivated victims accessing the hotline. We don't have in Australia a charity fraud resource such as they do in the United Kingdom where the Charity Commission for England and Wales has a special tie-in arrangement with the National Fraud Authority. Through that resource the UK Charities Commission recently reported that the money lost to charity fraudsters could be as big as £2 billion.[406]

The chapter then examined the issue of charity fraud from several perspectives including failure in moral leadership. Although the research is not available yet, it might be the case that the peculiarities of charity organisations, compared to say a business, makes them especially vulnerable to the moral failings of leadership. Two cases studied in the book, the RSL case (Chapter Four) and the Sharobeem case (Chapter Five) made it very clear that the moral climate of a charity relies on the ethical character of its CEO. As the old saying goes, "the fish rots from the head down". When there are no extra eyes on CEO conduct the charity can stay rogue for a considerable time. In the Chapter Five case, Sharobeem benefited for years from a zombie board and a government regulator asleep in the wheelhouse.

Other dimensions of the charity fraud phenomenon: high volunteer component, extensive financial illiteracy, zombie boards and low level of suspicion towards people who advocate worthy causes were explored to the conclusion that charities (big and small) have by their nature a special vulnerability to fraud.

It was also important to spotlight the new charity regulator, the Australian Charities and Not-for-profits Commission. Unfortunately, the analysis that followed was not that charitable. It was in two parts: a look at the Commission's history, structure and activities, and an ideological profile of its leader, Gary Johns.

The standout fact that came from this research was how under-resourced the Commission is. With only seventeen full time staff in the compliance area the Commission must rely on unevaluated proactive measures, unevaluated risk management strategies, and the most troubling of all, a reliance on self-reporting by charities as to what they are up to. Charities, especially the big ones, we should know by now, have no problem in tendering false or exaggerated information to the regulator.

The Chapter also raised the question, what is the Chair of the Commission, Gary Johns, up to? His career from a moderately left Labor Party minister to a central place in the most prominent right wing think tank in Australia, the Institute of Public Affairs, is interesting because it ideologically follows the same path taken by charity from a high-presence government model to a model of market welfare. Johns was characterised as the man of the moment because the government has put him into the Commissioner's chair as a safe pair of hands to manage the transition of the charity landscape to one of market welfare.

With the stage suitably choreographed with history, the state of charity, including current controversies, and a critical eye cast over the charity regulator, the time was right to bring the fraud cases onto the stage. The cases were chosen because each of them had been through investigations of the highest forensic integrity and their details were now in the public arena.

The Shane Warne Foundation was the subject of an investigation by Consumer Affairs Victoria. Two things make the Shane

Warne Foundation different from the other cases profiled here. First, there was no finding of fraud. Secondly, Consumer Affairs Victoria did their investigation in secret, and, despite my attempt through freedom of information laws to obtain it, at the time of writing this material remains locked away. The attraction of this case was that it was a perfect example of the weaknesses in what I call the *celebrity charity* model.

The celebrity charity model, by its nature, has its own unique flaws. The public, specifically the donating public, are content to see these charities in the same light as they see the charismatic person who started them. Public trust in these charities is instant and unassailable by negative facts. So even when the media is running hot with stories of fraud and mismanagement in these charities, donations still come in because people won't believe that the charismatic person is capable of anything but good works. Even regulators tread warily. One reason I was given as to why my appeal to the Victorian Information Commissioner was taking so much time, and well outside the legislated response times, was that he had to be careful because the subject of the appeal was Shane Warne.

While celebrity charities can use star quality to avoid or evade accountability with respect to performance and the management of donated funds, the iconic charities face a different set of flaws. The New South Wales RSL was the subject of an inquiry by the NSW Legislative Assembly (Bergin Inquiry) and one of the fraudsters in that case has been charged by police and is facing court. Iconic charities are uniquely placed to convert history into public trust. RSL National has been in existence since 1916. RSL LifeCare is even older, having been established in 1911. With over 100 years' service to the ex-digger community it is little wonder that the donating public may feel safe that their money is going to the right place.

RSLs share this historical space with other hallowed charities which have been around for a long time such as the St. Vincent de Paul Society (1854), Anglicare (1857), Benevolent Society (1834) and the Australian Red Cross (1914). These historical charities have built up enormous reservoirs of trust. Times are changing. Where once the community extended an enormous latitude to these charities, now, their high approval may no longer be a firewall against public disapproval and reputational damage. The RSL charity fraud case profiled in this book has contributed significantly to the view that hallowed charities can go bad. The threshold is coming down for these charities.

The Kate Amanda Smith case which ended in a jail sentence after she pleaded guilty in the Southport District Court was offered as an example of, probably, the most common charity fraud model, the key player model. All that is required for charity fraud to occur in this model is for one person to go bad and exploit sleeping audits, zombie boards, colleagues not reporting for fear of repercussions, and trust in the fraudulent operator. We do keep coming back to trust a lot in this analysis.

The Sharobeem case was an extended treatment of the key player charity fraud model because of the vast amount of material available. Based on seventeen days of evidence taking, twenty one witnesses and two thousand, three hundred and ten pages of transcripts, the Sharobeem study is probably the largest study of Australian charity fraud ever published. Sharobeem was found guilty in September 2018 and is, at time of writing, awaiting a decision from the NSW Director of Public Prosecutions as to whether she will face trial and possible imprisonment.

Of all the cases profiled here, Sharobeem's was the most egregious. I can sum it up in one crime among hundreds: she bought a Mercedes car for her husband with charity funds. Many matters had to be in conjunction for this gross charity fraud to occur. In the table below Sharobeem "scored" on seven of the ten preconditions for charity fraud to occur. She "reported" to a hand-picked board who were in awe of her. She was a media darling and was in all the outlets and seen around Sydney at big events rubbing shoulders with the Premier of the state and other notables. She had a strong, intimidating attitude to her cowed staff, many of whom were former refugees. She always knew that a thorough audit would see her undone. That's why she avoided such an audit until it was too late. Finally, it was a forensic audit ordered by her board just waking up, that exposed her. Greed is the beguilingly simple reason she stole charity money. She loved the good life for herself, her husband and her two sons. There was also regulatory failure by the audit and risk management parts of the two NSW state departments that annually sent her grants. Finally, she justified stealing the money on the false excuse that she had worked so hard for the charities with only an average remuneration in return. Even she did not believe this, and it was rejected by ICAC.

In the final table Figure 9 on the next page, the insights gained from the cases are distilled into the preconditions for charity fraud to occur. The only conditions that ticked all the boxes were the absence of regulatory scrutiny and audit failure. All the charities case studied here had these types of failures. It is important to understand how these regulatory and audit functions need to be alive to the possibility of fraud and coordinate with each other.

The next most common pre-condition for charity fraud was unbridled greed in the principal operators, or as in the case of the RSL NSW, a conspiracy of principals. Audits and regulatory scrutiny have a part to play in picking up greed. Also going into this mix would be lifestyle checking. Eman Sharobeem was noted for her expensive jewellery, dresses, makeup and holidays. To the acute observer these were things she could not afford on her salary.

The celebrity fact comes next as a fraud pre-condition. Shane Warne and Eman Sharobeem were the only ones who fitted this bill, and Warne was never charged with fraud. What celebrity does is to lull the public. Celebrity means being heard and seen a lot. On those occasions, the opportunities are there to explain to a gullible audience what you are doing in the charity and how it is making a difference.

Evidence of an intimidated workplace was only found in the charities that Sharobeem controlled. Likewise, evidence of a dishonest board was only found in the RSL NSW case, which also registered historical trust as a pre-condition for fraud.

Evidence of secretive boards whereby high sources of agency authority do not give up information about their operations was only found in the Shane Warne Foundation and the RSL NSW.

Only one agency had strong evidence that the fraud occurred under the very noses of a board, and that was the Sharobeem matter.

Finally, to the question of, "Why are you taking this money that does not belong to you"? Two agencies gave clear evidence that the fraud was sanitised in the mind of the fraudsters by excuses such as a long and un-remunerated volunteer service prior to being

Precondition	Shane Warne Foundation	RSL NSW	Amanda Smith	Eman Sharobeem
Secretive Board	✓	✓		
Zombie Board				✓
Dishonest Board		✓		
Intimidated Workplace				✓
Audit Failure	✓	✓	✓	✓
Greed		✓	✓	✓
Regulatory Failure	✓	✓	✓	✓
Celebrity Factor	✓			✓
Historical Trust		✓		
Stolen Money*		✓		✓

Figure 9. Preconditions for Charity Fraud and Mismanagement.
*Stolen money in lieu of hard work, underpay or prior years as a volunteer

paid (RSL NSW) or in compensation for a low salary and long overtime activities (Sharobeem).

Ashforth and Vikas' model of the normalisation of corruption was first mentioned in the RSL case, considered above, and it is worth revisiting as a final insight.

The authors present three mutually reinforcing processes: *institutionalisation,* where an initial corrupt decision or act becomes embedded in the workplace culture and thereby routinised; *rationalisation*, where the illegality is sanitised to justify and perhaps even valorise corruption; and finally *socialisation*, where naive newcomers are induced to view corruption as permissible, if not desirable. This model is highly relevant to considerations of charity fraud because it centres corruption on people who regard themselves, and are regarded, as good people, hence their alignment with charity work. The model, the authors say:

> … helps explain how otherwise morally upright individuals can routinely engage in corruption without experiencing conflict, how corruption can persist despite the turnover of its initial practitioners, how seemingly rational organizations can engage in suicidal corruption and how an emphasis on the individual as evildoer misses the point that systems and individuals are mutually reinforcing.[407]

The Ashforth and Vikas model emphasises the *social* nature of morality. It sees the workplace not as a moral vacuum which has ethics injected into it through staff who "walk" their personal moral frameworks into the workspace. Rather, this space sets up its own moral code. To the outsider, such as a charity regulator, this code instantly looks distorted if it is not practising its core service values. To the insider the workplace moral code is not necessarily distorted, it's just the way it is.

We can layer this reasoning by thinking about dual moral codes: one for home and one for work. This explains the puzzle we call moral contradiction. A person can take their moral bearings from the workplace and steal charity funds but enforce the Eighth Commandment to his or her children at home.

While this line of scholarship explains how good people cross ethical lines at work, we need another dimension. In their recent study, Moore and Gino also offer a framework that identifies *social* reasons why our ethics can be highjacked by the prevailing workplace (im)moral code.[408] The authors do a great service in this regard by identifying three processes: moral neglect, moral justification, and immoral action. We can think of *moral neglect* in two ways. First, a person-centred way, whereby the staff member is a moral "lightweight" in the sense that the needle on their moral compass is erratic and subject to fluctuations governed by self-serving ambitions. *Moral justification* refers to the existence of powerful narratives at the individual and organisational levels that reference self-serving frameworks to justify bad behaviour. The third way is to see moral neglect in organisational terms. *Immoral action* is when the whole organisation acts to moral standards well below community expectations.

How can we sum up our travels through the *land of giving?* It is not an easy place to understand. Crazy quilt contradictions, paradoxes and hypocrisies are visible everywhere we travelled. Various groups with opposed needs and purposes populate this land, often indifferent to the others' existence. It is a land of good-intentioned, compassionate people who donate to and work in good causes. These are the best Australians. They dedicate themselves to righting wrongs, giving the downtrodden access to justice, food, shelter and education.

New groups with undocumented social, medical and economic needs appear in clearings in our consciousness regularly, seeking help, guidance and recognition. They co-habit these sites and compete with groups who have been seeking care and attention for many years (think Aboriginal youth suicide).

It is a land where the rules of the jungle apply. A conflict zone where big charities, hard-pressed and desperate for funds, compete with mosquito-sized charities for the fickle charity dollar.

Meanwhile new groups of people migrate to its shores with the purpose of making a buck out of the misfortune of others. Into this land come crooks and psychopaths who have broken free of their moral moorings, if they existed in the first place. These people insinuate themselves into charities and suck them dry. The Sharobeem case in Chapter Five comes to mind.

Lining up at passport control to get into this troubled land we also see the professional fund raisers who take most of the money collected by chuggers for their own greedy purposes. In the queue coming last, because they are new to the land, are the philanthropic trusts. These tax-avoidance and reputation precious entities, cleverly set up by the best corporate accounting brains in the business, are also keen to make a buck out of good intentions. Professional fund raisers, philanthropic trusts, charitable foundations, corporate tax lawyers and charity governance consultants, are swarming ashore like carpetbaggers after the American Civil War.

Buzzing around all this is a charity regulator too small for its purpose, too narrow in its scope and headed by a person who has made some remarkably anti-charity comments in the past, to the extent of our having to question his fitness for this role. This unfitness for office extends to the current Commissioner's punitive view on advocacy charities. Most charities keep their heads down and never criticize government social policies for fear of being de-registered for tax deductibility purposes. The few who do, as we considered in the section on advocacy charities, get special attention from the regulator. The Commission was given an extra $1 million in the 2018–19 budget as a war chest in readiness for any future appeal from a charity de-registered allegedly because its advocacy behaviour was a disqualifying act.

What can we do with this hindsight? First, we must get rid of the Australian Charities and Not-for-profits Commission. It's got the wrong genetics. In its previous iteration it was a backroom section in the Australian Tax Office where a few bureaucrats busied themselves with qualifying charities for tax relief. It's a Commission that has been brought up under our tax laws when it should be a child of redistributive justice and egalitarianism.

Not only should the charity regulator be abolished, we should wipe out the regulator's *raison d'être*. All tax advantages for charities and philanthropic trusts should be stopped, pending a complete review of the Commonwealth *Charities Act 2013*. This review should cut away all charitable purposes and return the definition of charity back to its Samaritan roots. I acknowledge that vested corporate interests will have to be neutralised to get to this goal. Recall the figures presented in the Introduction: tax concessions to charities and tax concessions to donors amount to $1.3 billion per year. So much good could be done with this money by governments interested in social justice. Also recall the tax benefits philanthropic trusts receive. Between 2001 and 2009 these trusts slugged the tax paying community $935.68 million in tax benefits. This is *more than double* the $461.77 million that the trusts returned to the community in grants! Fifty percent return on investment, nice.

So, in my wild utopianism, the charity regulator goes. Tax deductibility on donations to charities go; and we put a bomb under the definition of "charities" and "charitable purposes". These definitions are tarmac-wide and very floppy. I can see the logic of recognising, say, the St. Vincent de Paul Society as a charity and I can see how its works are specifically for "charitable purposes". But, try as I might, I cannot see why the Wesley College in Victoria is a registered charity, thereby able to claim massive tax deductions. The college had an income of $104.6 million in 2017. It is currently engaged in a colossal renovation program that includes $21 million for a music school, $16 million for a boarding facility, and $2.5 million to refurbish its boathouse. Just down the road, Caulfield Grammar, another registered charity, with income of $95.1 million, is constructing a new aquatic centre that will have an Olympic-sized swimming pool, with moveable floors and walls and so-called "wellbeing spaces" for dance, pilates, meditation and yoga. Along with Haileybury College, Victoria and Knox Grammar School in New South Wales, these four schools are Australia's richest schools and, together, spent more on new facilities and renovations than the poorest 1,800 schools combined. Wesley College, Haileybury College and Caulfield Grammar in Melbourne, together with Knox Grammar in Sydney, spent $402 million. They teach fewer than 13,000 students. The poorest 1,800 schools spent less than $370 million. They teach 107,000 students.[409]

One of Australia's poorest schools is Sheidow Park Primary School in South Australia. At the end of each school year, the principal Jennie-Marie Gorman, takes a walk around the school with the finance officer and the groundsperson. They pass windows held together by safety screens; they inspect the playgrounds built twenty years ago; they note the walls that haven't been painted in fifteen years; and they look again at the patch of exposed concrete in the front office, where the finance officer's swivel chair has worn a hole in the carpet. That hole will be fixed in about five years, if all goes to schedule. "We have a plan to carpet two to three classrooms a year, based on need, so the ones with the biggest holes in them or the biggest rips get replaced first", Ms Gorman says. "We also need new carpet in the office, but we look at what the children need first and we put ourselves at the end of the line — which is just normal teacher stuff. That's just how we operate".[410]

The conclusion here is obvious. The charity concession to non-government schools is propping up a massive two-class system, with all the dreadful inequities, managerial opacity and fraud that this implies. The answer? Disallow schools and universities (including Australia's largest charity, Melbourne University), from registering as charities for tax deduction purposes.

The same should be said for religious organisations. As the section on Charitable Activities recognised, 32% of all registered

Charites are religious organisations. The second largest charity in Australia is the Catholic Archdiocese of Brisbane. Centrecare, the Archdiocese's welfare arm has an active and genuine charity mandate. But should tax-deductibility be used for church infrastructure, staff training, insurance discounting and the like?

Similarly, the mega rich Hillsong Church, mentor to this year's Prime Minister, Scott Morrison, has at least twelve separate registrations on the charity regulator's register. It pulls in over $80 million dollars a year in tax-free revenue.[411] Where is all this tax-free money going? Does the regulator know? I doubt it.

The solution to these massive inequities is to cancel charitable status for all churches and educational organisations (as a start). That's 51% of all current charities. Imagine the savings to revenue that could be directed to social welfare for the disadvantaged. Religious organisations, schools, universities and the like would have to re-register and apply for tax benefits for those parts of their organisations *directly* involved in ministering to the needs of the disadvantaged. Cancelling registered charity status would also mean that a religious organisation like Hillsong could get tax relief if it runs food services for the poor, for example, but not for the purchase of goods and services unrelated to social welfare.

If we wipe out tax advantages for donors, charities and trusts we have detonated the ACNC's current statutory reason for existence: to register charities for taxation purposes. As we saw in the section "The Shut-Eyed Sentries", the Commission only has seventeen people in its compliance division and twenty-seven people registering charities.[412] That tells us where the priorities are. Its other roles are peripheral to this one. Sure, the Commission says it is also about detecting abuse in the system. But how can it do this? Parliament has given it adequate investigative power but insufficient staff to exercise these powers. Fake charities, incompetent charities, pointless charities and corrupt charities swarm this troubled land. Yet what is our charity regulator doing about this?

Developing a new charity regulator unhinged from the anti-distributive tax regime and matched up to the genuine fair-go aspirations in the Australian community would mean remodelling the regulator as a hybrid combination of the philosophy and practice of two Commissions, the Australian Human Rights

Commission and the Australian Aged Care Quality and Safety Commission. All charities, trusts and not-for-profit organisations would need to operate under registration from this new Commission.

The new style of registration would shift from the old game of organisations squeezing themselves into one or the other "charitable purpose" to get the tax deductions to an outcome focussed culture. Two books by the American author, Robert Lupton, also drive home this view. In *Toxic Charity*, Lupton brilliantly argued that while charity makes donors feel better, he asks "... what would charity look like if we instead measured it by its ability to alleviate poverty and needs?"[413] If you say you are in the business of alleviating homelessness, you need to prove that to the new regulator annually to be eligible for continuing registration. And you won't be able to prove what social impacts you have made by simply writing a report, as happens now, asserting the fact.[414] Your performance will need to be evaluated externally by a hands-off authority such as the highly credible Australian Council of Social Service.

Once we have blocked tax deductibility, once we have narrowed the concept of charity back to its Samaritan heritage, once we have done this, carpetbaggers like Melbourne University and Caulfield Grammar School will leave the scene.

Then we should start law reform to make charity fraud a special type of offence in the State and Commonwealth criminal codes. Harsher penalties should apply to first offence charity fraudsters, as there is usually never a second offence. Fraudsters should be held under lifetime guarantees to pay the stolen money back. This guarantee should extend to the beneficiaries of fraudsters' wills.

Finally, we must bring the state back in. Yes, as I shift uncomfortably in my chair, knowing what's coming, I am talking about a resurgent socialism free of its Marxist bondage, that puts a moral obligation back on governments to spend more, do more and feel more, for our vulnerable Australians.

Maybe then will disadvantaged Australians get a fair go. Maybe then when Alan and Lisa meet (remember them from page 12) they will meet as true equals.

William De Maria

William De Maria has had a dissent-rich academic career. He graduated at top of his class with an Honours Degree from the University of New South Wales in 1970. He was New South Wales' first community social worker. Then, the first social planner in New South Wales when he joined the Special Projects Team in the Town Planning Department at Bankstown Council. He was subsequently Director of Social Planning for the Riverina Council for Social Development under the fabled Australian Assistance Plan. After returning from time overseas on a Churchill Fellowship, he joined the School of Social Work at the University of Queensland in 1978 before its reputation was smashed. He completed his Master of Social Work there in 1980 and his PhD in Australian welfare history in 1988.

Never one to luxuriate in his ivory cell, William co-founded the Brisbane Welfare Rights Centre and in 1999 established the Queensland Whistleblowers' Action Group. One claim to fame is that (for a while) he got away with teaching radical social work to students at the University of Queensland. This was at a time when dissent was a career-busting activity at the same University that gave former Premier, Joh Bjelke Petersen, an honorary degree.

With two books, chapters in three other books and sixty refereed journal articles, he has an extensive national and international publishing record. He has won awards for his academic publications. He conducted the inaugural whistleblowing research in Australia and his *Deadly Disclosures: Whistleblowing and the Ethical Meltdown in Australia* was published to wide acclaim in 1999 by Wakefield Press. His controversial thirty-three-year career at the University of Queensland has been profiled recently in *Radicals in Australian Social Work* (Connor Court 2017).

Like most activists, he bears the scars. When the University of Queensland tried to sack him he took his case to the powerful Commonwealth Parliamentary Privileges Committee and won resoundingly. For the first time in Commonwealth legal history a university was found to be in contempt of parliament for its treatment of a faculty member.

Over the years he has had numerous other appointments, most notably a ten-year stint on the Administrative Appeals Tribunal. He has been a regular media commentator and, when not doing these sorts of things, breeds Belted Galloway cattle.

Endnotes

Online access occurred March 2018–October 2019

1. Australian Charities and Not-for-profits Commission, *Annual Report,* 2017–18, "Registration Outcomes". See also McLeod, J., *JB Were Cause Report,* "20 years of (r)evolution in the not-for-profit sector", April 2016. https://www.jbwere.com.au/content/dam/jbwere/documents/the-cause-report.pdf, p. 4.
2. Toynbee, P., "Behold the Tory leadership candidates: all in denial, all in dreamland", *The Guardian,* 11 June 2019.
3. Australian Council of Superannuation Investors Ltd, *CEO Pay in ASX 200 Companies, 2018,* September 2019. https://www.acsi.org.au/publications-1/research-reports.html
4. University of Melbourne, Melbourne Institute, HILDA Survey 2018. https://melbourneinstitute.unimelb.edu.au/hilda
5. Henriques-Gomez, L., "Newstart and life on $40 a day. 'It's not living its surviving'", *The Guardian,* 16 August 2019. https://www.theguardian.com/australia-news/2019/aug/17/newstart-and-life-on-40-a-day-its-not-living-its-surviving?CMP=Share_AndroidApp_Email
6. Australian Bureau of Census, "Census reveals a rise in the rate of homelessness in Australia". https://www.abs.gov.au/ausstats/abs@nsf/lookup/2049.0Media%20Release12016. The ABS defines someone as homeless if their current living arrangement is in a dwelling that is inadequate, has no tenure and does not allow control of and access to space for social relations.
7. Davey, M., & Knaus, C., "Homelessness in Australia up 14% in 5 years, ABS says", *The Guardian,* 14 March 2018. https://www.theguardian.com/australia-news/2018/mar/14/homelessness-in-australia-up-14-in-five-years-abs-says
8. This figure was, with technical assistance from the Australian Charities and Not-for-profits Commission, accessed on 11 June 2019 from the vast datadotgov data set.
9. Butcher, J.R., "The rise of big charity in Australia", paper delivered to the Association for Research on Non-profit Organisations and Voluntary Action (ARNOVA) Conference, Denver Co., November 2014. https://www.researchgate.net/publication/271197473_The_rise_of_Big_Charity_in_Australia.
10. Backus, P., & Clifford, D., "Are big charities becoming more dominant? Cross-sectional and longitudinal perspectives", *Journal of the Royal Statistical Society,* Vol. 176, Issue 3, 2013; Kay, L. 2016, "Small charities struggling while their larger counterparts grow", *Third Sector,* quoted in https://senscot.net/small-charities-struggling-while-their-larger-counterparts-grow-ncvo-figures-show/; Kay, L., Faulkner, M. & Nguyen, C., "Celebrity charities just compete with all other charities – so why start one"? *The Conversation,* 31 January 2017. https://theconversation.com
11. Klapdor, M., & Arthur, D., "Welfare – What does it cost"? Commonwealth

Government Parliamentary Library, 2016. https://www.aph.gov.au/About_Parliament/Parliamentary_Departments/Parliamentary_Library/pubs/BriefingBook45p/WelfareCost
12. This argument follows closely the work done by Klapdor & Arthur, ibid.
13. Ibid.
14. St. Vincent de Paul Society, Federal Budget Priority Statement 2018. https://www.vinnies.org.au/page/Publications/National/Articles
15. The Pharmaceutical Benefits Scheme began as a limited scheme in 1948, with free medicines for pensioners and a list of 139 "life-saving and disease preventing" medicines free of charge for others in the community. In 2017–18 an average of 804,000 scripts for subsidised medicines were filled every day. Australian Government Department of Health, *Annual Report*, 2017–18, p. 5.
16. The "rich" in this context are people earning in excess of $200,000 pa. "High-income earners would receive $77 billion in tax cuts under the Liberal plan", *The Guardian*, 18 April 2019. https://www.theguardian.com/australia-news/2019/apr/18/high-income-earners-would-receive-77bn-in-tax-cuts-under-liberal-plan
17. Shiel and Stilwell, quoting recent Evatt Foundation figures, say that "... the poorest 40% of Australian households effectively have no wealth at all: about half of them actually have negative net wealth because of their personal debts. At the opposite pole, the wealthiest 10% have more than half the nation's total household wealth. The top 1% alone have at least 15% of the total wealth", Shiel, C., & Stilwell, F., "Land of the 'fair go' no more: wealth in Australia is becoming more unequal", *The Conversation*, 8 August 2016. https://theconversation.com/land-of-the-fair-go-no-more-wealth-in-australia-is-becoming-more-unequal-63327
18. Bregman, R., *Utopia for Realists. And how we can get there,* Bloomsbury, New York, 2016.
19. "Rutger Bregman, the Dutch historian who went viral", *BBC News*, 31 January 2019, https://www.bbc.co.uk/news/av/world-47077624/rutger-bregman-the-dutch-historian-who-went-viral
20. Wibawa, T., "How the world's richest 1 per cent may be fuelling the problems they're trying to help solve", *ABC News*, 28 June 2019. https://www.abc.net.au/news/2019-06-28/philanthropy-donations-may-fuel-problem-its-trying-to-solve/11199102
21. Ibid.
22. Martin, F., "The Socio-Political and Legal History of the Tax Deduction for Donations to Charities in Australia", *Adelaide Law Review*, Vol. 38, 2017, pp. 1–28.
23. Reich, R., *Just Giving. Why Philanthropy is failing Democracy and how it could do better,* Princeton University Press, 2018.
24. Dalton, B., & Cham, E. "Australia's rich give little – and a culture of secrecy surrounds their philanthropy", *The Conversation*, 17 August 2016. https://theconversation.com/australias-rich-give-little-and-a-culture-of-secrecy-surrounds-their-philanthropy-63879

25. PAFs were part of the Howard Government's response to the report on philanthropy in Australia by the Business and Community Partnerships Working Group on Taxation Reform dated 26 March 1999. See Australian Government, The Treasury, "Improving the Integrity of Prescribed Private Funds", Discussion paper, November 2008, point 5, p. 1. http://www.treasury.gov.au/sites/default/files/2019-03/Prescribed_Private_Funds.pdf
26. Cham, E., "Philanthropic foundations cost taxpayers – and so should be made accountable", *UTS Newsroom,* http://newsroom.uts.edu.au/news/2016/10/philanthropic-foundations-cost-taxpayers-%E2%80%93-and-so-should-be-made-accountable
27. Ibid.
28. Dalton & Cham, op. cit.
29. Section 51 of the Australian Constitution grants the Commonwealth legislative power. Prior to this amendment the only social services provision was s51(xxiii) that gave power to legislate for invalid and old-age pensions. The 1946 Australian referendum introduced s51(xxiiiA), which reads: "The provision of maternity allowances, widows' pensions, child endowment, unemployment, pharmaceutical, sickness and hospital benefits, medical and dental services (but not so as to authorise any form of civil conscription), benefits to students and family allowances."
30. For substantial critiques of the neoliberal catastrophe see; Davies, W., *The Limits of Neoliberalism,* Sage, London, 2016; Harvey, D., *A Brief History of Neoliberalism*. Oxford: Oxford University Press, 2005; Harvey, D., "Neoliberalism as Creative Destruction", *The Annals of the American Academy*, 2007, Vol. 610, pp.22–44; Chomsky, N., *Profit over People – Neoliberalism and Global Order*. New York, Seven Stories Press, 1999.
31. This is an international development. See for example, Estes, R., & Zhou, H., "A conceptual approach to the creation of public-private partnerships in social welfare", *International Journal of Social Welfare*, Vol. 24, No. 4, December 2014, pp. 348–363.
32. The classic texts here are; Titmuss, R., "The Social Division of Welfare", in *Essays on the Welfare State*, Allen & Unwin, London, 1963; Tawney, RH., *Equality*, Unwin Books, 1931. See also, Shapiro, D., "Egalitarianism and welfare-state re-distribution", *Social Philosophy and Policy*, Vol. 19, No. 1, January 2002, pp. 1–35; Spicker, P., *Equality and Welfare. An Introduction to Social Policy*, http://spicker.uk/social-policy/equality/htm.
33. Although I am not being critical of the job being done, there is a New Zealand charity that is called Gap Filler. See https://gapfiller.org.nz/donate/
34. Reich, R., op. cit.
35. Ryan, F., "Mind the Gap. How Charities are Mopping up after the Government's Failure to Care", *New Statesman*, 5 February 2015. https://www.newstatesman.com/politics/2015/02/mind-gap-how-charities-are-mopping-after-government-s-failure-care

36. The point recognises that charities have multiple regulatory accountabilities.
37. Declaration, that woman is my wife.
38. Catholic Psychiatry Pastoral Care, http://www.cppc.net.au
39. This is despite the claim the Catholic Foundation makes that "gifts to Centacare directly benefit Centacare's Pastoral Ministries, which rely on the generosity of donors and volunteers". https://catholicfoundation.org.au/about-us/our-history/
40. To pursue this point further see: Schervish, P., "The Moral Biography of Wealth: Philosophical Reflections on the Foundation of Philanthropy", *Non-Profit and Voluntary Sector Quarterly*, 2006, pp. 1–10. https://www.bc.edu/content/dam/files/research_sites/cwp/pdf/moralbiography.pdf. See also Schervish, P., "Major Donors, Major Motives: The People and Purposes behind Major Gifts". *New Directions for Philanthropic Fundraising: Developing Major Gifts*, Vol. 16, 1997, pp. 85–112.
41. In 1970 Australia's population was 12.51 million. On 7 August 2018 Australia reached the 25 million mark. *ABC News*, 7 August 2018. For research on a comparison between Australia now and in the past see; Bain, P., Krooenberg, P., & Kashima, Y., "Cultural Beliefs about Cultural Change", *Journal of Cross-Cultural Psychology*, 46: 5, pp. 635–651, 2015.
42. St. Vincent de Paul is the patron saint of charity.
43. Wikipedia, "Eddy Groves". https://en.m.wikipedia.org›wiki›Eddy.
44. Rowse, T., *Nugget Coombs: A Reforming Life*, Cambridge University Press, 2002.
45. Gary Johns, ACNC Chair, refers to registered charities as the "market". Senate Economic Legislation Committee, 28 February 2018.
46. The Royal Commission into Aged Care Quality and Safety was established 8 October 2018. It must report by 30 April 2020, unless given an extension. Up until 12 September 2019 it has received 6022 submissions. The most common term of reference at the Commission in September 2019 was "substandard or unsafe aged care services". https://agedcare.royalcommission.gov.au/Pages/default.aspx
47. Categorising IWHS and NESH is a challenging exercise. Were they, until their demise, charities, as understood in the *Charities Act, 2013*, or were they not-for-profit organisations? A not-for-profit is an organisation that reinvests all of its profits back into itself to continue carrying out its mission. Not-for-profits can legally make a profit, but these profits can only be used for activities such as carrying out the day to day work of the organisation, paying tightly regulated staff wages, building infrastructure, or launching projects. Importantly, all of these activities must be congruent with the organisation's mission. Even if a not-for-profit closes, voluntarily or otherwise, profits cannot be claimed by the owners or the group's members. Instead, they must be redistributed to an organisation with similar goals. This definition does not seem to apply to IWHS or NESH. They did not make a profit (thanks to the actions of Eman Sharobeem). But possibly they were not allowed to make a profit

under the terms of the engagement with their sole funders: two NSW State Departments and one or two local government entities around Fairfield. On advice from ACNC on 6 August 2018, it seems that if IWHS and NESH carried out charitable purposes under the *Charities Act* and abided by other stipulations in that Act, then they could have registered as charities, notwithstanding the fact that they did not solicit or receive donations or bequests. So, both organisations in this study are treated as registerable charities.

48. https://libquotes.com/christopher-smart
49. For that see: Dickey, B., *No Charity There: A Short History of Social Welfare in Australia*, Thomas Nelson, Melbourne, 1980; Kennedy, R. (ed), *Australian Welfare History: Critical Essays*, Macmillan, South Melbourne, 1982; Kennedy, R., *Charity Warfare: The Charity Organisation Society in Colonial Melbourne*, Hyland House, Melbourne, 1985; Lawrence, R., *Professional Social Work in Australia*, Australian National University, Canberra, 1965; Lawrence, R., "Australian social work: in historical, international and social welfare context", in Boas, P., & Crawley, J. (eds), *Social Work in Australia: Responses to a Changing Context*, Australian International Press and Publications, Melbourne, 1976, pp. 1–37.
50. McLeod, J., *op. cit.*
51. Freudenberg, G., *A Certain Grandeur: Gough Whitlam's Life in Politics*, Viking, 2009; Hocking, J., *Gough Whitlam: A Moment in History*, The Miegunyah Press, 2008; Kelly, P., *The Dismissal*, Angus & Robertson Publishers, 1983.
52. The *Poor Relief Act 1601* was not finally removed from the statute books until 1967 with the passing of the *General Rate Act*. https://en.wikipedia.org/wiki/Act_for_the_Relief_of_the_Poor_1601#References.
53. The *Poor Relief Act 1662* was an Act of the Cavalier Parliament of England. It was *an Act for the Better Relief of the Poor of this Kingdom* and is also known as the Settlement Act or, more honestly, the Settlement and Removal Act. The purpose of the Act was to establish the parish to which a person belonged (i.e. his/her place of "settlement"), and hence clarify which parish was responsible for him should he become in need of Poor Relief (or "chargeable" to the parish poor rates). This was the first occasion when a document proving domicile became statutory: these were called "settlement certificates". https://en.wikipedia.org/wiki/Poor_Relief_Act_1662.
54. Lawrence, R.J., *Professional Social Work in Australia*, Ch. 2 (ANU eView, an imprint of ANU Press). This is a reprint from Lawrence's classic account of the history of Australian social work, published in 1965.
55. Ibid.
56. Ibid., Lawrence's research discovered that the paper was given by the Rev. Alexander Macully, M.A., "The Unemployed", See *Proceedings of the First Australian Conference on Charity*, Melbourne, 1890, pp. 114–9.
57. The role of State Governments in social policy in this period is acknowledged but not considered. Suffice to say that the enactment of

Commonwealth legislation for old age pensions and invalid pensions superseded the old-age pensions introduced by New South Wales and Victoria (1901) and Queensland (1908), and the invalid pensions introduced in New South Wales (1908).

58. Kewley, T., *Social Security in Australia*, Sydney University Press, 1965; Lawrence, J., op. cit.; Herscovitch, A., & Stanton, D., "History of Social Security in Australia", *Family Matters*, No. 80, 2008, p. 51.
59. The Royal Commission into Social Insurance sat from September 1923 to October 1927.
60. Lawrence, op. cit., Chapter 2.
61. *WebsterWorld Encyclopaedia of Australia*. http://www.websterworld.com/websterworld/aust/1/1939wareconomysetback193.html
62. The National Welfare Scheme was to be financed from a £30,000 fund. The funded programs were: new maternity benefits, funeral benefits for old age and invalid pensioners, unemployment and sickness benefit, increase in the maternity allowance and old age and invalid pensions, widows' pension and payments for dental, medical and health costs.
63. De Maria, W., "From Battlefield to Breadline. The State of Charity, 1938–1945," PhD, University of Queensland, 1988.
64. In a short three-year period, the Whitlam Government managed to enact a large volume of highly significant social legislation including: Medibank, supporting mothers' benefit, Australian Assistance Plan, Race Discrimination Act, free university education, Family Court, Australian Legal Aid Office, Aboriginal land rights.
65. John Maynard Keynes was one of the most influential economists of the twentieth century. He proposed a macro-economic theory that endorsed a strong interventionist role for governments in ironing out the boom-bust cycles in capitalist economies. So plausible was his approach that it was adopted by most post-World War II developed countries. His theory started to wane in the 1970s.
66. The Organisation for Economic Co-operation and Development (OECD) is an intergovernmental economic organisation with 36 member countries founded in 1961 to stimulate economic progress and world trade. Social expenditure comprises cash benefits, direct in-kind provision of goods and services, and tax breaks with social purposes. To be considered "social", programmes must involve either redistribution of resources across households or compulsory participation. Social benefits are classified as public when general government (that is central, state, and local governments, including social security funds) controls the relevant financial flows. All social benefits not provided by general government are considered private. OECD, *Social Spending, 2016*. https://data.oecd.org/socialexp/social-spending.htm
67. Staples, J., "Democracy resides in participation in organisations", Green Agenda Essay, 5 September 2015, *Green Agenda*. https://greenagenda.org.au/2015/09/democracy-resides-in-participation-in-organisations/
68. Buchman, FN., *Remaking the world, The Speeches of Frank Buchman*,

Blandford Press 1947, revised 1958, p. 46.

69. For discussion on the definition of charity see: Sheppard, I., Fitzgerald, R., Gonski, D., *Report of the Inquiry into the Definition of Charities and Related Organisations* (2001) ('*Sheppard Report*'). Canberra, Commonwealth Treasury. https://catalogue.nla.gov.au/Record/2630199. This Report is about definitional issues concerning charities and related entities, namely public benevolent institutions, religious institutions and community service organisations. The Committee's terms of reference required it to consider these matters in the context of Commonwealth law. Although that law is for the most part revenue law, this Report is not about the taxation treatment of charities and related entities.
70. *Charities Act*, 2013 (Cth), *Preamble*. Assented to 29 June 2013. Started on 1 January 2014.
71. Ibid, Part 2, Division 1.
72. Ibid, 2013, S11(b).
73. Ibid, 2013 (Cth), Part 3, Division 1.
74. ACNC advice to author, 26 July 2018.
75. On 8 November 2018 the ACNC deregistered the Islamic religious organisation Diwan al Dawla. The reasons for this decision remain a secret. However, it would be tied up with the very aggressive attitude of Diwan al Dawla that it is above Australian law.
76. Productivity Commission, *Contribution of the Not-for-Profit Sector,* Draft Report, October 2009, file:///C:/Users/daqui/Downloads/not-for-profit-draft.pdf., p. xxvi. See also interview with inaugural ACNC chair, Susan Pascoe, ABC Radio National, "Charities Commission Review", *Saturday Extra*, 30 September 2017 (Geraldine Doogue). http://www.abc.net.au/radionational/programs/saturday extra/charities-commission-review/8996792
77. The review of the *Charities Act* and the ACNC, *Strengthening for Purpose: The Australian Charities and Not-for-profits Commission Legislation Review*, was published on 31 May 2018. https://static.treasury.gov.au/uploads/sites/1/2018/08/p2018-t318031.pdf, Submission, ATO, 30 April 2018.
78. Ibid., Submission, ACNC, 19 January 2018, page 17. Most not-for-profits outside the regulatory ambit of ACNC self-assess their tax status and ability to access tax concessions through Business Activity Statements.
79. Even the Australian Bureau of Statistics conflates the meanings. Its database "8106.0. Not-for-Profit Organisations in Australia" is clearly only referring to registered charities.
80. Powell, A., Cortis, N., Ramia, I. & Marjolin, A., *Australian Charities Report 2016*. Centre for Social Impact and Social Policy Research Centre, UNSW Australia, 2017. https://mafiadoc.com/australian-charities-report-2016-acnc_5c3bf302097c470d6f8b45ae.html
81. We do, however, need to curb our reaction to these general figures because the ACNC definition of what is a charitable organisation is so

encompassing as to be useless for serious research purposes.

82. *Australian Charities Report,* Centre for Social Impact & Social Policy Research Centre, University of New South Wales, 2015. https://www.csi.edu.au/media/Australian_Charities_Report_2015_Web_ND8DU2P.pdf
83. Queensland Sugar Limited, "What We Do". https://www.qsl.com.au/what-we-do
84. Queensland Sugar Limited, *Annual Activity Statement,* 2018 to ACNC. https://www.acnc.gov.au/charity/9381fcfaf0d1256c97f32b0e7c053e9e#ais-640be74902cfc753eaf9dfa53e2ba130
85. Australians take in 95.6 grams of sugar every day which is almost 4 times the maximum recommendation set by the WHO. https://www.worldatlas.com/articles/top-sugar-consuming-nations-in-the-world.html
86. Powell, A., Cortis, N., Young, A., Reeve, R., Simnett, R., & Ramia, I., *Australia's Smallest Charities 2015.* Centre for Social Impact and Social Policy Research Centre, UNSW Australia, 2016. https://apo.org.au/sites/default/files/resource-files/2017/05/apo-nid76249-1226026.pdf
87. Ibid., p. 1.
88. Ibid.
89. Ibid.
90. Tony Nicholson quoted in Butcher, op. cit.
91. Butcher, op. cit. For Butcher big charities are large, multi-service, national social service organisations.
92. ACCC, *Research into Commission-based Fundraising in the Australian Charity Sector,* 2017, p. 17. https://www.accc.gov.au/media-release/report-on-commission-based-fundraising-in-the-charity-sector
93. *Giving Australia,* Australian Centre for Philanthropy and Non-Profit Studies, Queensland University of Technology, 2016. https://www.philanthropy.org.au/about-us/giving-australia/
94. National Australia Bank, *Charitable Giving Index,* various years, https://business.nab.com.au
95. ACCC, *Research into Commission-based Fundraising in the Australian Charity Sector,* 2017, op. cit., p. 8.
96. Before ACNC, the registration of charities for tax purposes was conducted by the Australian Taxation Office.
97. Aid/Watch was exempt from income Tax liability under the Income Tax Assessment Act 1997 from 2000 and from fringe benefit tax and GST from 2005.
98. *Aid/Watch Incorporated v Commissioner of Taxation* [2010] HCA 42. 1 December 2010. See also Chia, J., Harding, M., O'Connell, A., "Navigating the Politics of Charity. Reflections on the Aid/Watch Inc. v Federal Taxation Commissioner", *UMelb LRS, 9.*
99. *Charities Bill 2013,* second reading, 29 May 2013. http://parlinfo.aph.gov.au/
100. Explanatory memorandum to the *Charities Bill 2013,* paragraphs 1.107–1.108.

101 Staples, J., "Incredulous disbelief as Gary Johns to head charity

regulator", 12 September 2017. https://johnmenadue.com/joan-staples-incredulous-disbelief-at-gary-johns-to-head-charities-regulator/

102 House of Representatives Standing Committee on Community Affairs, 1991, *You have your moments: Report on Funding of Peak Health and Community Organisations*, AGPS, Canberra, p. 17–18.

103. It is hard to decide whether it is ignorance or mendacity when right wing politicians wrongly depict advocacy groups who are upsetting them as charities. Eric Abetz, a leading right winger in the Turnbull Government often accuses the national advocacy group GetUp! Of being a charity, when it is clearly not.

104. Karp, P., "'Bizarre overreach': charities fear regulator wants to control their spending", *The Guardian*, 23 January 2018. https://www.theguardian.com/australia-news/2018/jan/24/bizarre-overreach-charities-fear-regulator-wants-to-control-their-spending

105. Extract from transcript, Senate Economic Legislation Committee, 28 February 2018.

106. ACNC, "ACNC receives additional funding in 2018-19 Federal Budget", https://www.acnc.gov.au/media/news/acnc-receives-additional-funding-2018-19-federal-budget

107. "Archbishops to question PM over future of Catholic charity", *The Australian*, 15 July 2018. https://www.theaustralian.com.au/national-affairs/archbishops-to-question-pm-over-future-of-catholic-charity/news-story/f5e7959833a70ae1cf4845186b2ba34d

108. "Ged Kearney and Bill Shorten celebrate victory in Batman", *ABC News*, 26 March 2018, http://www.abc.net.au/news/2018-03-26/ged-kearney-and-bill-shorten-celebrate-batman-victory/9586206

109. As quoted in *The Australian*, 15 July 2018.

110. ACNC, "Advocacy by charities", http://www.acnc.gov.au/ACNC/Register_my_charity/Who_can_register/What_char_purp/ACNC/Reg/Advocacy.aspx

111. "Anti-church standover not on", *The Australian*, "Editorial", 14 July 2018. https://www.acnc.gov.au/ACNC/Comms/LN/LN_20180718.aspx?TemplateType=P

112. *Strengthening for Purpose*, op. cit.

113. Australian Christian Lobby, *Election Day Western Australia*. https://www.acl.org.au/election_day_wa The Australian Christian Lobby (ACL) was back in the news in mid-2019 when they took over the collection of donations for the legal fighting fund of former Wallaby star Israel Folau who was sacked by Rugby Australia for his homophobic comments. More than two million dollars was raised in the first two days of the appeal. This action prompted a number of complaints to the Australian Charities and Not-for-Profits Commission alleging ACL was receiving tax-deductible donations for a purpose outside its core mission. *The Guardian*, 27 June 2019. https://www.theguardian.com/sport/2019/jun/26/israel-folau-acl-australian-christian-lobbys-fundraising-sparks-complaints-to-watchdog

114. The big donations from Rinehart's Hancock Prospecting to the IPA only came to light in the NSW Supreme Court on subpoena as a result of a long-running battle between Rinehart and her estranged daughter, Bianca. Readfearn, G., "Gina Rinehart company revealed as $4.5m donor to climate sceptic thinktank", *The Guardian*, 20 July 2018.
115. IPA, "About". https://ipa.org.au/about-ipa
116. ACNC, "Charity subtypes and charitable purposes", http://www.acnc.gov.au/ACNC/Reg/TypesCharPurp.aspx
117. The Evatt Foundation is named after Herbert Vere Evatt. He served as leader of the Australian Labor Party and Leader of the Opposition from 1951 to 1960, Attorney-General and Minister for External Affairs from 1941 to 1949, and as a judge of the High Court of Australia from 1930 to 1940. The Foundation describes itself as "... a non-profit organisation dedicated to upholding the ideals of the Australian labour movement: social justice, equality, democracy and human rights." https://evatt.org.au
118. The ACNC inherited charity records from the Australian Taxation Office (ATO) after 2012. The ATO records in comparison to ACNC records were quite rudimentary. Registered charities are now required to report annually. This in itself could be an important vetting process, but it suffers the usual flaws associated with self-reporting.
119. Martin, l., "Israel Folau: Australian Christian Lobby's fundraising sparks complaints to watchdog", *The Guardian*, 26 June 2019. https://www.theguardian.com/sport/2019/jun/26/israel-folau-acl-australian-christian-lobbys-fundraising-sparks-complaints-to-watchdog?CMP=Share_AndroidApp_Email
120. Nicholson, T., "Speech on the Future of the Community Welfare Sector", Brotherhood of St. Laurence, 27 May 2014, pp. 3–4. http://library.bsl.org.au/jspui/bitstream/1/5804/1/Tony_Nicholson_speech_on_community_welfare_sector_27_May_2014.pdf
121. Ibid., p. 4.
122. Ibid.
123. Ibid., pp. 5–6.
124. "Charities look to business for inspiration", *Australian Business Intelligence,* 18 February, 2002. https://trove.nla.gov.au/work/97521111?q=charity-business+model&c=article&versionId=110879176
125. The fact that two of the three case examples featured here are not eligible for charity registration, as they are profit making entities, is irrelevant to the exposé of the flaws in the charity-business paradigm.
126. Rana, M., & Lea, L., "Save the Children 'failed' to deal with women's complaint". https://www.bbc.com/news/uk-43287838, 7 March 2018.
127. McCambridge, R., "Running a charity like a business? Save the Children UK reinforces old lessons", *Non-Profit Quarterly*, 16 July 2018. https://nonprofitquarterly.org/2018/07/16/running-a-charity-like-a-business-save-the-children-uk-reinforces-old-lessons/

128. Ibid.
129. Ibid.
130. Save the Children UK, "Our Board of Trustees". www.savethechildren.org.uk
131. Andy Ricketts, "Save the Children UK chair to step down early after investigation", Third Sector, 21 December 2018, www.thirdsector.co.uk
132. *ABC News*, "Bupa aged care home audit reveals multiple failings including assaults on residents". https://www.abc.net.au/news/2019-09-12/bupa-seaforth-inquiry-exposes-multiple-failings/11506332
133. As is usual in these situations, the regulator, the Aged Care Quality and Safety Commission, knew where the smell was coming from but kept its insights tightly to itself under convenient FOI exemption and restrictive privacy policies.
134. Australian Associated Press, "Bupa aged care boss vows snap inspections of nursing homes", 16 September 2019. https://www.theguardian.com/australia-news/2019/sep/16/bupa-aged-care-boss-vows-snap-inspections-of-nursing-homes?CMP=Share_AndroidApp_Email
135. De Maria, W., "After the Scandal. Recovery Options for Damaged Organisations", *Journal of Management & Organisation*, Vol. 16, Issue 1, March 2010, pp. 66–82.
136. Bupa.com.au/mbf.
137. Lafrenz, C., "Bupa Australia to pay $157m to ATO", *Financial Review*, 8 March 2019. https://www.afr.com/companies/healthcare-and-fitness/bupa-australia-to-pay-157m-to-ato-20190308-h1c55b. One of the filings stated that the tax authority was scrutinising Bupa's approach to "thin capitalisation" — the practice of using loans between different corporate entities within the same group to artificially reduce a company's tax burden.
138. Martin, l., "Bupa defence health contract: warning lives could be at risk over referrals logjam", *The Guardian*, 13 September 2019. https://www.theguardian.com/australia-news/2019/sep/14/bupa-defence-health-contract-warning-lives-could-be-at-risk-over-referrals-logjam?CMP=Share_AndroidApp_Email
139. https://www.bupa.com/Corporate/our-performance/financial-results
140. http://www.earlehavenretirement.com.au
141. Private nursing homes are not registerable entities with the Australian Charities & Not-for-profits Commission.
142. Royal Commission into Aged Care Quality & Safety (henceforth RCACQS), Transcript of evidence, 5 August 2019. https://agedcare.royalcommission.gov.au/hearings/Pages/Transcripts.aspx#brisbane-hearing
143. Australian Associated Press, "Crying, screaming and violent threats after aged care home closed, inquiry told", *The Guardian*, 5 August 2019. https://www.theguardian.com/australia-news/2019/aug/05/crying-screaming-and-violent-threats-after-aged-care-home-closed-inquiry-told
144. Australian Associated Press, "Abuse claims aired at Earle Haven Inquiry",

https://www.agedcareinsite.com.au/2019/09/abuse-claims-aired-at-earle-haven-inquiry/

145. Ibid.
146. Ibid.
147. Ibid.
148. Ibid.
149. Ibid.
150. RCACQS, Transcript, pp. 4208–4215.
151. RCACQS, Transcript, pp. 4236–4247.
152. http://www.bakertilly.com/insights/emerging-trends-in-not-for-profit-fraud
153. The head of power for the ACCC is the *Competition & Consumer Act*, 2010.
154. https://www.scamwatch.gov.au/types-of-scams/fake-charities
155. BDO Australia, *Not-for-Profit Fraud Survey*. https://www.bdo.com.au/en-au/insights/surveys/not-for-profit/bdo-not-for-profit-fraud-survey-2014
156. http://www.bakertilly.com/insights/emerging-trends-in-not-for-profit-fraud/
157. Ibid.
158. Nguyen, K., "Street Fundraisers raised $120 million for Australian charities in 2018, report reveals", *ABC News*, 4 January 2019. https://www.abc.net.au/news/2019-01-04/charity-street-fundraisers-raise-plenty-of-money-report-reveals/10614810
159. Ibid.
160. Brown, R., & Whitbourne, M., "Charities' fundraising costs swallow millions in donations", *Sydney Morning Herald*, 21 December 2013. https://www.smh.com.au/national/charities-fund-raising-costs-swallow-millions-in-donations-20131220-2zqyw.html
161. Ibid.
162. Ibid.
163. Nguyen, K., op. cit.
164. *Sydney Morning Herald*, 28 November 2017.
165. *Bywater v Appco Group Australia Pty. Ltd.* [2018] FCA 707 (18 May 2018).
166. *ABC News*, 18 May 2018. While 1400 were signed into the class action by late 2016, it is reported that this number could balloon to between 4000 and 8000 affected employees. (Statement by Rory Markham, of Chamberlains Lawyers, *ABC News*, 22 October 2016).
167. Adero Law Firm, https://appcoclassaction.com.
168. *ABC News*, 22 October 2016.
169. *Daily Telegraph*, 19 June 2017.
170. *Daily Telegraph*, 19 June 2017. As a result of airing these comments Appco sued Channel 7 in the Federal Court. See Battersby, L., "Appco suing Seven Network for 'malicious falsehood' over Sunday Night", *Sydney Morning Herald*, 7 July 2017. https://www.smh.com.au/business/companies/appco-suing-seven-network-for-malicious-falsehood-over-sunday-night-20170706-gx5vl5.html
171. *Australian Charities & Not-for-profits Commission Act*, 2012.

172. Staples, J., "Incredulous disbelief", op. cit.
173. ACNC Bill, Revised Explanatory Memorandum, paragraph 1.3.
174. By way of accountability its decisions can be appealed to the Administrative Appeals Tribunal and the courts and it is answerable to the Parliament, Commonwealth Ombudsman, Auditor-General and the Australian Information Commissioner.
175. *ACNC Annual Report*, 2017–8, Table 4.6. https://www.acnc.gov.au/tools/reports/acnc-annual-report-2017-2018
176. This is a full-time equivalent figure.
177. The under-resourcing of government commissions is a widespread and serious problem. For example, the 2019-20 New South Wales budget provided decreased allocations to the Independent Commission against Corruption (ICAC), the Information and Privacy Commissioner, the NSW Ombudsman and the NSW Law Enforcement Conduct Commission. ICAC's staffing levels, meanwhile, are at near-record lows, according to the most recent figures. Average staffing was 104.96 and 98.07 full-time equivalents in 2017–18 and 2016–17 respectively, well below the levels seen prior to 2015–16. ICAC's staffing peaked at 126.4 full-time staff in 2013–14. The number of matters received by ICAC – including public complaints, referrals, and own-motion investigations – has climbed from 2,436 to 2,751 in the past two financial years. *The Guardian*, 24 June 2019. https://www.theguardian.com/australia-news/2019/jun/25/nsw-accused-of-starving-icac-and-integrity-watchdogs-of-funding?
178. See G. Johns, "Addressing the Risk of Misuse in the Charity Sector". Paper presented to the 7th Australian Public Sector Anti-Corruption Conference, Melbourne, 30 October 2019, Slide 6.
179. Ibid.
180. ACNC, *Charity Compliance Report*, 2018, p. 15. file:///C:/Users/daqui/Downloads/charity_compliance_report_2018 _0%20(1).pdf, figure 6.3.
181. ACNC, *Annual Report*, 2017–2018, Tables 4.7, 4.8. On 30 June 2018 ACNC had 84 full-time equivalent employees, of which 16.60 FTEs were in the compliance unit. https://www.acnc.gov.au/tools/reports/acnc-annual-report-2017-2018. The Commission lost 3 of these FTEs in the 2018–19 Budget.
182. ACNC, media release, 29 May 2018.
183. South Australian Department of Consumer and Business Services. https://www.charities.sa.gov.au/charities_details.php?licenceNo=CCP3131¤t=Yes
184. The charity was Catholic Education Melbourne. The ACNC denies the charge.
185. *ACNC Act*, Chapter 4. https://www.legislation.gov.au/Details/C2012A00168
186. Commonwealth Senate, Economic Legislation Committee, Estimates, Treasury Portfolio, 28 February 2018. file:///C:/Users/daqui/Downloads/report.pdf
187. ACNC, *Annual Report*, 2016–17, Table 3.1. https://www.acnc.gov.au/tools/

reports/acnc-annual-report-2016-17.

188. ACNC, *Annual Report*, 2017–18, Table 3.1. https://www.acnc.gov.au/tools/reports/acnc-annual-report-2017-2018
189. ACNC reviews and investigations "will be confidential and no information about a case will be published". *ACNC Act*, ss 40–5(2), 40–10(2)(a). The new ACNC commissioner, Dr Gary Johns, is on record as disapproving of these privacy restrictions. See ACNC, *Charity Compliance Report*, 2017, p. 3.
190. Other Commonwealth regulators such as: Australian Prudential Regulatory Authority, Australian Securities and Investments Commission and the Australian Competition and Consumer Commission have far greater discretion with respect to making their investigations public.
191. ACNC, *Annual Report*, 2017–18, op. cit., Table 4.1.
192. *Strengthening for Purpose: The Australian Charities and Not-for-Profits Commission Legislation Review*, was published on 31 May 2018. Recommendation 18 suggests the ACNC Commissioner be given the discretion to disclose information about investigations into charities. https://static.treasury.gov.au/uploads/sites/1/2018/08/p2018-t318031.pdf
193. ACNC advice to author, 30 August 2018.
194. *Strengthening for Purpose*, op. cit., Recommendation 16. There is also provision for charities (other than basic religious organisations) to apply to the ACNC to have information about them withheld from the charity register. In 2016–17, 807 charities were allowed, for various reasons, to keep details of themselves off the register. *ACNC Annual Report*, 2016–17, Table 3.3.
195. *Associations Incorporation Act* 1981 (Qld) s59.
196. *Associations Incorporations Act* 1985 (SA) s 35.
197. For a discussion of this see Vaughan-Williams, J., "The Future of Charity Regulation in Australia: Complexities of Change", *Adelaide Law Review*, 2016, 37(1): 219–246.
198. Johns, G., "Addressing the Risk of Misuse in the Charity Sector", op. cit., slide 3.
199. I wish I had been the first to say this. Alas, it is David Marr's wonderful description of Sir Garfield Barwick.
200. Evans, G., *Inside the Hawke Keating Government: A Cabinet Diary*, Melbourne University Publishing, 2014; Kelly, P., *The Hawke Ascendency*, Allen & Unwin; Kelly, P., *The End of Certainty*, Allen & Unwin, 2008; Martin, S.P., "Labor and Financial Deregulation: The hawke-Keating Government, banking and New Labor", PhD Thesis, University of Wollongong, 1999. https://trove.nla.gov.au/work/26604109?q=hawke-keating+government&c=book&versionId=32039081
201. The banks were ushered into a new deregulated environment. It would take another 25 years before Australia would be told, from evidence to the 2018 Royal Commission into Banking, how socially destructive this deregulation was. Royal Commission into Misconduct in the

Banking, Superannuation and Financial Services Industry. Established 14 December 2017. Final report handed down 1 February 2019. https://financialservices.royalcommission.gov.au/Pages/reports.aspx#final

202. Simple statistics tell all. At the start of the Hawke-Keating Government in 1983 the corporate tax rate was 49%. In March 2017 this was brought down by the Turnbull Government to 25% for companies with an annual turnover of up to $50 million. The base company tax rate in 2019 was 27.5%. https://www.ato.gov.au/Rates/Company-tax/

203. The Institute of Public Affairs was started in 1943 as a big business reaction to the demise of the United Australia Party, the forerunner of the Australian Liberal Party. IPA's priority was to ensure a place for business in the post-World War II reconstruction and act as an ideological counterpoint to Keynesianism and Socialism. The founders of IPA Victoria included the inaugural chairman, G.J. Coles, Chairman of Directors of GJ Coles & Co., H.G. Darling, Chairman of Directors, The Broken Hill Pty. Co., Sir Keith Murdoch, Chairman of Directors, *The Herald & Weekly Times* and W.I. Potter, Founder of the stockbroking firm, Ian Potter & Co.

204. Staples, J., op. cit. Australian Institute of Progress. https://aip.asn.au

205. Gambaro, T., "Launch of *The Charity Ball*", Speech at Alliance Hotel, Spring Hill, 14 July 2015, Australian Institute for Progress. https://aip.asn.au/2015/07/launch-of-the-charity-ball/

206. Howard, J., "The Liberal Tradition: The Beliefs and Values Which Guide the Federal Government", *Menzies Lecture*, 1996, Sir Robert Menzies Lecture Trust. www.menzieslecture.org/1996, p. 2; Staples, J., "NGOs out in the cold: The Howard Government policy towards NGOs", Discussion paper 19/6, 2006, Democratic Audit of Australia. www.joanstaples.org/publications.

207. Staples, J., "Incredulous disbelief at Gary Johns to head charity regulator", 12 December 2017, in John Menadue, *Pearls and Irritations*. https://johnmenadue.com/joan-staples-incredulous-disbelief-at-gary-johns-to-head-charities-regulator/. Staples says: "The idea for a *Protocol* was initiated by the IPA. When the proposal was put to the Howard Government, it was accepted with no tender, no public announcement and no adherence to National Audit Office guidelines, which require selection criteria or evaluation of the consultants. The ABC Radio National's *Background Briefing* pointed out the irony of the IPA, which did not disclose its donors, contracting in secret to monitor NGOs for their transparency and accountability – a fact that seems to have been lost on both the Howard Government and the IPA".

208. In December 2017 (the same month as Johns' appointment as ACNC Chair), the government announced the terms of reference for the 5-year review of the *Australian Charities and Not-for-profits Act* 2012 (Cth) and the *Australian Charities and Not-for-profits Commission (Consequential and Transitional) Act* 2012 (Cth).

209. Karp P., op. cit.

210. “Anti-charity campaigner new head of charity regulator”, Community Councils of Australia. www.community council.com.au
211. Staples, J., “Incredulous disbelief”, op. cit.
212. Ibid.
213. Ibid.
214. Ibid.
215. https://www.allgreatquotes.com/quote-197685
216. For biographies of Warne with varying degrees of subjectivity see: Jackson, I., *Shane Warne*, Cambridge UP, 2000; Browne, A., *Shane Warne*, Heinemann, 1998; Warne, S., and Ray, M., *Shane Warne: My own Story*, Bookman Publishers, 1997.
217. Nielsen, B., and Keane, D., “Shane Warne lends name to Jurassic-era volcanoes a kilometre beneath the earth”, *ABC News*, 14 August 2019. https://www.abc.net.au/news/2019-08-14/cricket-legend-shane-warne-lends-name-to-jurassic-era-volcanoes/11411934
218. Steve Waugh Foundation. https://stevewaughfoundation.com.au
219. According to Wikipedia, Andrew Forrest and his wife Nicola were the first Australians to pledge the majority of their wealth to charities in their lifetime. They do this through endowments such as the Minderoo Foundation and the Walk Free Foundation.
220. *Sydney Morning Herald*, 14 February 2016.
221. Another report has Shane Warne’s brother receiving $210,000 in salary for an executive position with the Foundation. *Daily Mail Australia*, 30 November 2015. https://www.dailymail.co.uk/home/sitemaparchive/day_20151130.html
222. *Sydney Morning Herald*, 14 February 2016.
223. Warne refuted the claim on his Facebook page stating, “We have raised 7.8 million dollars so far, our total give to over 125 different children’s charities will be 4.1 million dollars and that equates to 51–52% of revenue raised we have given away to those charities.”
224. *Sydney Morning Herald*, 14 February 2016.
225. Press release from Simon Cohen, Director of Consumer Affairs Victoria, 25 February 2016. file:///C:/Users/daqui/AppData/Local/Packages/Microsoft.MicrosoftEdge_8wekyb3d8bbwe/TempState/Downloads/The%20Shane%20Warne%20Foundation%20Public%20statement%2026%20February%202016%20(1).pdf
226. *ABC News*, 12 March 2016.
227. Ibid.
228. *Herald Sun*, 10 May 2016.
229. *Herald Sun*, 17 August 2016.
230. *ABC News*, 11 January 2017.
231. Fundraising in NSW requires charities to distribute above 35% to beneficiaries or face de-registration. *ABC News*, 11 January 2017.
232. These figures are from the Shane Warne Foundation 2016 audited report submitted to the ACNC on 20 December 2016.
233. On 5 March 2018 the Victorian Commission for Gambling and Liquor

Regulation revealed that it had commenced disciplinary proceedings against Crown Casino for illegal tampering with its betting machines. *ABC News*, 5 March 2018. Previously Crown Casino was fined $300,000 for removing betting options on 17 of its poker machines without approval. On 3 August 2018 the regulator renewed Crown Casino's licence but found serious issues of governance. See also Dowling, J., "Crown property jewel cost $1 a year", *Sydney Morning Herald,* 12 September, 2008. https://www.smh.com.au/national/crowns-property-jewel-costs-1-a-year-20080911-4eru.html

234. Shane Warne Foundation 2014 audited report submitted to the ACNC on 19 February 2015.
235. Ibid.
236. Commercial Real Estate, www.commercialrealestate.com.au
237. Report of the Inquiry under the *Charitable Fundraising Act 1991* into The Returned and Services League of Australia (New South Wales Branch), RSL Welfare and Benevolent Institution and RSL LifeCare Limited. January 2018. https://www.finance.nsw.gov.au/sites/default/files/inquiry_report_cfa.pdf., point 8.4.46.
238. Castello, R., & Smith, S., "South Australian RSL put into administration only two weeks before Anzac Day", *Adelaide Advertiser*, 13 April 2017.
239. ACNC, "RSL Queensland Commits to Rectify Serious Governance Failures", Media statement, 29 March 2018, Number 235. http://www.acnc.gov.au/ACNC/Comms/Med_R/MR_235.aspx
240. ACNC, Media Release #241, 20 July 2018, "RSL National President Steps Down". http://www.acnc.gov.au/ACNC/Comms/Med_R/MR_241.aspx
241. RSL LifeCare operates retirement living and residential aged care services throughout New South Wales and the Australian Capital Territory. The organisation serves 7,500 residents and clients, employs over 3000 staff and operates from 50 locations.
242. The Royal Commission into Institutional Responses to Child Sexual Abuse was a Royal Commission established in 2013 by the Australian Government pursuant to the *Royal Commissions Act 1902* to inquire into historical allegations of sexual abuse in church and secular welfare agencies. It went from 13 January 2013 to 15 December 2017.
243. *Sydney Morning Herald*, 17 January 2017.
244. Report of the Inquiry under the *Charitable Fundraising Act 1991* into The Returned and Services League of Australia (New South Wales Branch), RSL Welfare and Benevolent Institution and RSL LifeCare Limited. January 2018. https://www.finance.nsw.gov.au/sites/default/files/inquiry_report_cfa.pdf. Between 15 May 2017 and 10 November 2017, 105 Notices or Summonses were served on various entities and persons. There were four private hearing days and 32 public hearing days with a total of 35 witnesses who gave evidence in the public hearings of the Inquiry. Henceforth Bergin Inquiry.
245. Ibid., point 8.1.2.
246. Ibid., point 1.6.

247. Ibid., points 1.13, 1.16.
248. Ibid., point 1.27.
249. Ibid., point 1.29.
250. Ibid., point 8.4.30. This was for the period December 2009–November 2014.
251. Ibid., point 2.46. For the period 16 December 2008–21 November 2014
252. Ibid., point 8.4.28. The period was November 2008–November 2014.
253. Ibid., point 8.4.4.
254. Ibid., point 8.4.6.
255. Ibid., point 8.4.17. The period the son stayed in the State President's suite was 2007–2014.
256. Ibid., point 8.3.17.
257. Ibid., point 2.21.
258. Audio recording of State Council meeting, 27 January 2015. Ibid., point 8.3.14.
259. Ibid., point 2.4.
260. Ibid., point 2.41. Thirty one percent of Council members received "consultancy fees" in 2006 (4 of 13); 45% in 2007 (5 of 11); 78% in 2008 (7 of 9); 80% in 2009 (8 of 10); 90% in 2012 and 2016 (9 of 10); and 100% in 2010, 2011, and 2013 to 2015 (10 of 10 in 2015; and 9 of 9 otherwise).
261. Ashforth, B. & Vikas, A., "The Normalisation of Corruption in Organisations", *Research in Organisational Behaviour,* Vol. 25, 2003, pp. 1–52. See also Campbell, J., & Göritz, A., "Culture Corrupts! A Qualitative Study of Organizational Culture in Corrupt Organizations", *Journal of Business Ethics*, Vol. 120, No. 3, 2014, pp. 291–311.
262. Robertson, J., "Former RSL president Ken Doolan 'directed charity to cover up expenses scandal', inquiry told", *Sydney Morning Herald*, 27 September 2017.
263. Bergin Inquiry, point 8.3.80.
264. Wroe, D., "RSL investigates claim car given to former national president Ken Doolan", *Sydney Morning Herald*, 23 September 2017.
265. Lavoipierre, A., "RSL president Robert Dick defends parting gift to predecessor Ken Doolan", *ABC News,* 25 September 2017.
266. Third Sector, "RSL told to fix 'non-compliance' over gift", 8 March 2018. https://thirdsector.com.au
267. Ibid.
268. Bergin Inquiry, point 8.3.88.
269. Ibid., point 8.3.130.
270. Ibid., point 8.6.63. The State Councillors were Messrs Crosthwaite, Haines, Harrigan, Henderson, Humphreys, Hutchings, James, McManus-Smith, Metcalfe, Stephenson, Toussaint, White and Dr Bain.
271. In the period covered by the Terms of Inquiry the directors of RSL LifeCare who were paid consulting fees were Mr Kells (2007 to 2016); Mr White (State Councillor, Honorary Treasurer and State President of RSL NSW) (2007 to 2015); Mr Carlson (State Councillor of RSL NSW) (2008); Mr Riddington (2007 to 2016); Mr Longley (2007 to 2016); Mr Rowe

(State President of RSL NSW) (2010 to 2014); Dr Macri (2007 to 2016); Ms Mulliner (State Councillor and CFO of RSL NSW) (2009 to 2016); Mr Hardman (State Councillor RSL NSW) (2008 to 2011); Mr Crosthwaite (State Councillor of RSL NSW) (2007 to 2016); Mr Humphreys (State Councillor RSL NSW) (2011 to 2016); and Mr Murray (2015–2016). See Ibid., point 9.2.2.

272. Bergin Inquiry, op. cit., point 9.2.11.
273. Ibid., point 9.2.30.
274. Ibid., point 9.2.38.
275. Ibid., point 9.2.43.
276. Ibid., point 9.2.55.
277. Ibid., point 9.2.56.
278. Ibid., point 9.2.75.
279. Ibid., point 9.2.119.
280. Ibid., point 9.2.123.
281. Ibid., point 9.2.136.
282. Ibid., point 9.2.136.
283. These were: Carlson, Crosthwaite, Hardman, Harrigan, Humphreys, Kells, Longley, Macri, Murray, Mulliner, Riddington, Rowe and White.
284 Bergin Inquiry, op. cit., point 9.3.62.
285. Ibid., point. 9.3.110.
286. Ibid., point 9.3.111.
287. Ibid., point 9.4.108.
288. Ibid., point 9.3.116.
289. Ibid., point 9.3.134.
290. Ibid., section 9.4. Those referred were Crosthwaite, Kells, Longley (former Liberal member for Pittwater), Macri, Riddington, Rowe and White.
291. Pearson, A., "The moment Gerroa's Glenn Kolomeitz knew something was amiss within NSW RSL", *Illawarra Mercury*, 20 May 2017.
292. Ibid.
293. Ibid.
294. Lavoipierre, A., "RSL NSW denies silencing whistleblower over firing of chief executive", *ABC News*, 3 May 2017.
295. R v Smith 2016 1104 [1684], District Court of Queensland, Criminal Division, Bowskill, J. presiding. Matter heard 4 November 2016, p. 10.
296. Smart Employment Solutions Limited, *Annual Information Statement*, 2017.
297. Of its total gross income for 2016–17 the charity received $597,057 from government grants, $6.6 million as revenue for providing services, and $6,600 in donations and bequests.
298. R v Smith, op. cit., p. 11. The money Smith stole was withheld tax due to the ATO under the Pay-as-you-go (PAYG) arrangements.
299. *Queen v Amanda Kate Smith*, Statement of Facts, Point 12.
300. Ibid., point 17.
301. Ibid., point 33.
302. Ibid., point 34.

303. R v Smith, op. cit., p. 12.
304. Ibid., p. 13.
305. Ibid.
306. Ibid.
307. R v Smith, op.cit., sentence, 4 November 2016, p. 3.
308. *Filthy Rich & Homeless* was the most watched documentary series on SBS in 2017.
309. Screen Australia, Media Release, 16 January 2018. https://www.screenaustralia.gov.au/sa/media-centre/news/2018/01-16-over-3-million-invested-across-12-docos
310. This decision also defunded the two national housing peaks: National Shelter and the Community Housing Federation of Australia. Homelessness Australia closed its national office in early 2016. Homelessness Australia, *Homelessness Funding: A Quick Guide,* January 2016. https://www.homelessnessaustralia.org.au/sites/homelessnessaus/files/2017-07/Homelessnesss_funding_fact_sheet_UPDATED_Jan_2016.pdf
311. Foodora Facebook, 3 July 2017.
312. Powell, D., "As Foodora leaves Australia, who's left?" *Smart Company,* 3 August 2018. https://www.smartcompany.com.au/industries/hospitality/as-foodora-leaves-australia-whos-left-a-brief-history-of-australian-food-delivery-services/
313. This is a very rough estimate. The marker used was the sale in 2017 of a vacant multi-storey hotel at 9–25 Commonwealth St., Sydney for $70.5 million. The same building was sold in 2014 for $45 million. See Baume, M., "Hyde Park's $70.5 Million Dollar Sale", Core Logic. https://www.corelogic.com.au
314. New South Wales Independent Commission against Corruption, *Investigation into the Conduct of a Principal Officer of two Non-Government Organisations and Others*, September 2018. https://www.icac.nsw.gov.au/docman/investigations/reports/5311-investigation-into-the-conduct-of-a-principal-officer-of-two-non-government-organisations-and-others-operation-tarlo/file (henceforth Operation Tarlo, Final Report).
315. *Sydney Morning Herald,* 8 July 2017.
316. NSW Independent Commission Against Corruption, Operation Tarlo, transcript (T) 413. Henceforth TARLO.
317. TARLO, T499 (Schizophrenia), T420 (rape in marriage), T417 (description of husband).
318. 1987 is significant in Sharobeem's life for two other reasons. It was the year that Reginald Blanch became New South Wales' first Director of Public Prosecutions. Blanch would later conduct the ICAC investigation into Sharobeem's corruption. 1987 marked the start of IWHS, which was to be so inextricably woven into Sharobeem's life in the future.
319. TARLO, Exhibit 45.
320. Ibid., T420.

321. There are eleven Coptic churches within 20 kilometres of where Sharobeem was living in Parramatta. Each of these churches offered baptismal services.
322. TARLO, T422 (Priest buying airline tickets), T423 (Gamel's behaviour).
323. Ibid., Exhibit 29.
324. Ibid.
325. Ibid., T426.
326. The golden age of the Copts in Egypt came to an end in 1952 when Gamal Abdel Nasser overthrew the monarchy and kicked the British out. Since that time the Copt Christian minority has experienced the menace of discrimination and violence. None more so than after the overthrow of Mubarak and the rise of political Islam in 2011.
327. Ibid., Exhibit 30
328. Ibid.
329. Interview with Rachael Kohn, *The Spirit of Things*, Radio National, ABC Radio, 29 July 2012.
330. Hansen, S., "Suzanne Mubarak: Egypt's Mean Queen", *Newsweek*, 1 January 2012.
331. Ibid.
332. Ibid., T468-479.
333. Ibid., T915.
334. Ibid., T826.
335. Ibid., T729.
336. Ibid., T506.
337. Ibid., Exhibit 4.
338. Ibid., T506
339. Ibid., T839.
340. *NSW Legislative Assembly Hansard*, 21 August 2013. https://www.parliament.nsw.gov.au/Hansard/Pages/HansardFull.aspx
341. TARLO, op. cit., Mrdjenovic ICAC statement, point 28.
342. Ibid., T739.
343. Ibid., T754.
344. Ibid., T985.
345. Ibid., T784–T785.
346. Ibid., Maugeri statement, point 14.
347. TARLO, op. cit., T641.
348. Ibid, Boyd statement, point 29.
349. TARLO, op. cit., T506.
350. Ibid., T669, T673.
351. TARLO, statement from Marie Abboud, 6 December 2016.
352. Ibid.
353. Ibid.
354. Ibid.
355. TARLO, statement from Nathan Boyd, 20 December 2016, point 226.
356. TARLO, Chanthalangsy evidence, 3 May 2016, T237–238.
357. TARLO, statement from Watfa El-Bal, 1 February 2017, point 45.

358. TARLO, statement from Nevine Ghaly, 30 June 2016, point 42.
359. TARLO *Final Report*, p. 72. file:///C:/Users/daqui/Downloads/Investigation-into-the-conduct-of-a-principal-officer-of-two-non-government-organisations-and-others_Operation-Tarlo_Sep18%20(1).pdf
360. TARLO, Watton evidence, 1 May 2017, T2–T60.
361. TARLO, Paredo evidence, 2 May 2017, T103–T104.
362. TARLO, Lai evidence, 16 June 2017, T1094–T1101.
363. Ibid., T1141.
364. TARLO, Watton evidence, 1 May 2017, T43–T44.
365. The SWSLHD funded the IWHS for the periods from 2010–11 to 2014–15. Prior to this, IWHS had received funding from the SWSLHD's predecessor agencies. For the 2014–15 period, IWHS received $349,600 from the SWSLHD.
366. ICAC *Final Report*, p. 86.
367. Ibid., Chow statement, Exhibit 52, point 22.
368. Ibid., point 23.
369. Ibid., point 26.
370. TARLO, op. cit., T640.
371. TARLO, Ghaly statement, point 34.
372. Ibid.
373. TARLO, T641.
374. Hon. Sophie Cotsis, NSW Legislative Council Hansard, 28 May 2015. https://parliament.nsw.gov.au
375. TARLO, T1091.
376. Ibid.
377. TARLO, statement from Nevine Ghaly, 30 June 2016, point 53.
378. TARLO, Exhibit 44.
379. TARLO, T1023.
380. TARLO, evidence of Nathan Boyd, 4 May 2017.
381. TARLO, Damcevska-Stamenkovska statement, point 34.
382. For 2013–14, its last fully funded year, NESH received $362,447 from the NSW Department of Family and Community Services SW.
383. TARLO, Lai statement, point 54.
384. Pursuant to s10A of the *Criminal Assets Recovery Act, 1990.* The assets were: 66 Begovich Crescent, Abbotsbury, 51/36 Ainsworh Crescent, Wetherill Park, 4/87 Smart St., Fairfield, a property in Courallie Avenue Homebush West, 2004 Honda Accord, ANZ bank accounts. As mentioned, the order came 9 weeks too late for the money Charlie sent to Egypt.
385. IWHS was a not-for-profit non-government organisation women's health service, primarily funded by NSW Health via South West Sydney Local Health District, while the NESH was a not-for-profit NGO contracted and funded by the Department of Family and Community Services to provide affordable housing to women and children. In her capacity as CEO, Ms Sharobeem was a public official for the purposes of the *Independent Commission Against Corruption Act 1988.*

386. There were 17 days of evidence taking, 21 witnesses and 2310 pages of transcripts. Sharobeem gave evidence on 9 of those days.
387. Confabulation, in the psychiatric literature, refers to a person with a cognitive or neurological disability who distorts, fabricates or misinterprets memories without a conscious desire to lie and deceive.
388. The quotations are extracts from the TARLO transcripts.
389. TARLO, T1304.
390. Ibid., T780–920.
391. Ibid., T863–864.
392. Ibid., T842.
393. Ibid., T875–876.
394. Ibid., T914–916.
395. Ibid., T467–469.
396. TARLO, Sharobeem evidence, 10 May 2017, T573.
397. Ibid, T753.
398. TARLO, statement from Watfa El-Bal, 1 February 2017, point 6.
399. TARLO, Sharobeem evidence, 14 June 2017, T896–T915.
400. New South Wales Independent Commission against Corruption, *Investigation into the Conduct of a Principal Officer of two Non-Government Organisations and Others*, September 2018. https://www.icac.nsw.gov.au/docman/investigations/reports/5311-investigation-into-the-conduct-of-a-principal-officer-of-two-non-government-organisations-and-others-operation-tarlo/file
401. Ibid., p. 7–9.
402. Ibid., p. 25.
403. Murphy, J., "Charities attack 'fee-gouging' trustee companies", *Financial Review*, 14 January 2013. https://www.afr.com/politics/federal/charities-attack-fee-gouging-trustee-companies-20130114-jibcy
404. In 2018–19 the Charity Research Support Fund will receive £204 million for university-based charity research. https://www.amrc.org.uk/charity-research-support-fund-faqs
405. As at 11 June 2019.
406. Charity Commission of England and Wales, "Protect your charity form fraud and cyber-crime". https://www.gov.uk/guidance/protect-your-charity-from-fraud
407. Ashforth, B., & Vikas, A., op. cit., Abstract.
408. Moore, C. & Gino, F., "Ethically Adrift: How Others Pull our Moral Compass from True North and How can We Fix it"? *Research in Organisational Behaviour,* Vol. 33, 2013, pp. 53–77.
409. Ting, I., Palmer, A. & Scott, N., "Rich school, poor school: Australia's great education divide", *ABC News*, 6 September 2019. https://www.abc.net.au/news/2019-08-13/rich-school-poor-school-australias-great-education-divide/11383384. This brilliant example of investigative journalism used the *My School* finance databank.
410. Ibid.
411. Snow, D., "Inside the Hillsong Church's money-making machine", *Sydney*

Morning Herald, 13 November 2015. https://www.smh.com.au/lifestyle/inside-the-hillsong-churchs-moneymaking-machine-20151026-gkip53.html

412. These numbers are full-time equivalents.
413. Lupton, R., *Toxic Charity*, Harper One, New York, 2011. See also his *Charity Detox: what charity would look like if we cared about results?* Harper One, New York, 2015.
414. Gary Johns, the Charity Commissioner, has recently said that the ACNC is going to tighten up in this area by imposing a new set of questions in the Annual Activity Statements that charities file, requiring them to specify how they are helping people at the program level, rather than just at the organisational level. See Gary Johns, "Addressing the Risk of Misuse in the Charity Sector". Presentation to 7th Australian Public Sector Anti-Corruption Conference, Melbourne, 30 October 2019, slide 20.
415. ACNC 2016 AIS Dataset. https://data.gov.au/dataset/7e073d71-4eef-4f0c-921b-9880fb59b206/resource/b4a08924-af4f-4def-96f7-bf32ada7ee2b/download/datadotgov_ais16.zip

Index

D

E

F

G

H

I

Q

R

S

T

www.ingramcontent.com/pod-product-compliance
Ingram Content Group UK Ltd.
Pitfield, Milton Keynes, MK11 3LW, UK
UKHW042020190726
13854UKWH00005B/2383

9 780975 235256